D1018830

If Only My Family Understood Me...

a family can find new balance through stress

by Don Wegscheider

Foreword by Virginia Satir

Published by CompCare® publications

2415 Annapolis Lane, Suite 140, Minneapolis, Minnesota 55441
A division of Comprehensive Care Corporation

(Ask for our catalog, 800-328-3330, toll free outside Minnesota
or 612/559-4800, Minnesota residents.)

If Only My Family Understood Me . . .

Library of Congress Catalog Card
79-53160
ISBN No. 0-89638-038-5

5	6	7	8	9	10
86	87	88	89	90	91

To families . . .

> to the families I have worked with
> to the families I have learned from
> to the families I have relaxed with
> to the family I came from
> to the family I live in.

Contents

Editor's note: For the sake of continuity, each survival role in a family dealing with stress is exemplified in illustrations throughout the book by the same person. For instance, the Victim is shown as a man, the Protector as a woman, the Problem Child as an adolescent boy, the Forgotten Child as a gradeschool–age girl. These illustrations are not intended to be typical. Any of the survival roles described in the book may be assumed by any member of a family regardless of age or sex.

Foreword

This book offers a practical and fundamental way to see the process of the family in perspective. It helps to see both the foreground and background of the family in a balance which assists the reader in seeing the dynamic interplay between its moving parts. Extending our view to include the broader picture helps us to see our individual possibilities within the whole. I see the family unit as being a microcosm of the world, our planet.

Our planet is a whole. We know that. However, how many of us actually appreciate what that wholeness really means? We all know what a family is. But again, how do we appreciate the meaning of its wholeness?

Our planet is covered by a multitude of meridians and longitudinal lines. If we were to spread out this network on a flat surface it would be very easy to see that all lines are related to every other line, intersecting at regular and predictable intervals.

We, individuals in families and families as a unit, have a similar network, most of it present but unnoticed. If we see each intersection (person and parts of a person) as a point in joining the whole, and if we think of each point as being both an entry and exit, we might come up with the following conclusions:

1. There are very many of these points.
2. We are constituted physically so that we can focus on only one point at a time; there are always many more points present than we can see at any one moment in time.
3. In a lifetime we probably couldn't know them all in depth.
4. However, we could know that they all exist and that knowing one would extend the knowledge of the others.
5. If we could imagine that each point goes through to the center — the heart of the family — (thinking now in terms of the global shape), and that if we were to step inside and see where all the points meet, we

would see that, as we enrich and understand each point, we are contributing to an even larger center, bringing greater meaning and more resources.

There is an increasing number of books now being written concerning the family. Authors understandably write from their own experience, which is bound to differ, author to author. Because of the vastness and complexity of the family, there is probably no end to what we can discover. Each person who concerns himself or herself with the family is unique, and each family is unique. Therefore each family and the person guiding or observing has different contributions to make, depending on what they see and work out between and among them.

Don Wegscheider, in his book *If Only My Family Understood Me . . .,* adds such a dimension. From his personal warmth, understanding, and compassion and his experiences and appreciation of the family processes, we get both a fresh and expanded awareness of how to understand, view and implement family life so that it can move toward a more joyful and fulfilling experience for all concerned.

We will probably not ever know all of the various ways in which families can manifest themselves. Like the planet and its meridian and longitudinal network, we can always discover new points and new connections, both content– and process–wise, to deepen our understanding of what family life means for each person and how we can go about shaping new possibilities for it. In other words, Mr. Wegscheider's book confirms observations of what many of us have already seen, enriching these, adding new emphasis and translating the theory of what he presents in alternative useful ways, building a perspective which helps to keep the part and the whole in balance.

Virginia M. Satir
Family Therapist
Author of
Peoplemaking
Self Esteem
Conjoint Family Therapy
Making Contact
Your Many Faces

Author's Foreword

The spring of 1973 was an important time for me in my work with families. It was then that I went to a conference in Saskatoon, Canada, and studied with Virginia Satir, who formally introduced my wife, Sharon, and me to "family systems." Though studying with Virginia was exciting in itself, the high impact of meeting her was due largely to the context of our lives at the time. It was an experience that brought a lot of ideas into order.

Virginia has been truly a spiritual influence in our lives. She has brought us to new meanings. We are much indebted to Virginia for an awareness of the dynamics of the family system. At the Saskatoon Conference she gave us a base to start from. Her continued nurturing has spurred both of us to further applications of the model in our work. Virginia's and our missions match: to guide family systems to wholeness through congruence — that is, honest, open communication.

By 1972 I had been working with families in parish work in the Twin Cities for seven years. In the context of the Church I had a sense of mission and a direction to teach people a specific ideal and encourage them to bring their lives into harmony with that ideal. This became especially important in working with adults on live-in weekends. People were looking for inner growth. They were yearning to satisfy the hunger for discovering who they were and who God is.

In 1972 I also was in search of meaning — personal meaning. I did not doubt any of the true things outside of me, such as the Church theology or the people around me. I was struggling to see my personal place in the world around me. I needed to know where I fit. I needed more than just fitting into the roles at my disposal. I needed to learn how to take and to receive as well as to give. It was in 1972 that I made a career change which also became a major lifestyle change. That sense of relief, the sense of rightness indicated to me that though the style had indeed changed, the mission remained the same.

Sharon had been undergoing considerable growth and change before we came together in a relationship. Her work with adult groups and children's groups in the Church, her studies at the University of Minnesota and at Metropolitan Community College in Minneapolis had opened her eyes to many things, particularly her own gifts of perception and discernment in counseling and guiding others to a sense of wholeness.

Virginia Satir was the main influence in our putting into words what we had been feeling. Her counseling work with all members of the family together — or conjoint therapy — and her ways of describing families clarified our own thoughts. Channeling families' energies toward a growing self-worth became an expression of our mission. The mission needed more than enthusiasm; it needed some explicit goals for us and for the families we would help. The goal and concept of nurturing self-worth became a counseling model. The model grew and evolved from the base line contributed by Virginia and became the basis for Sharon's and my work in our respective agencies.

North Suburban Family Service Center in Coon Rapids, Minnesota, is an agency serving families in all sorts of stress, which may involve runaways, marriage, divorce, shoplifting, alcohol, illness, death. It is an agency serving all members of the family from age five and up. Besides being a direct service agency, North Suburban is also a teaching site for our counseling model. At the Center we see clients in relation to their families. The work we do is process-oriented rather than problem-solving. Our goal is to nurture self-worth, to reinforce the belief that families have enough energy to cope with most situations for themselves.

One day at the Center, I met a man named Ward Nerothin, a pastor of Elim Lutheran Church in Robbinsdale, Minnesota. Ward was a member of a group of community people who were taking field trips around the north suburbs of Minneapolis to look at human services agencies. He was at North Suburban that day, feeling a little guilty because he had missed the last few meetings of his group. An important obligation for a busy pastor is to know what is happening in the community.

During a presentation of North Suburban's program, Ward's interest perked up. Much of what I was describing was stirring the embers of a dream he had had for a long time.

I remember him asking, "Sure, you may be able to do it here, but can this type of program be reproduced successfully elsewhere?"

I said, "I know someone who is currently doing it." I gave him Sharon's name and address. He called her that same day.

When Ward and Sharon met, they found themselves finishing each other's sentences. The meeting of minds and spirits was the beginning of the agency in Robbinsdale called The House. In 1974, The House, a community counseling center, opened its door to families in stress. It was at this agency that many programs for children proved effective in bringing whole families to health.

One discovery common to both North Suburban and The House was the high incidence of chemical dependency among the clients. Most often this was not the reason for their coming, but was found to be the primary problem upsetting their family systems.

In 1976 Sharon accepted an invitation to become Director of Family Care at Johnson Institute in Minneapolis, a non-profit foundation which develops programs to foster the understanding and treatment of alcoholism/chemical dependency. There she narrowed her focus from families in general to chemically dependent families. What we knew to be true of all families could be used as a new basis for treating chemically dependent families. A description of her application of the model to chemically dependent families is available in the pamphlet, *Family Trap*.

In 1975 Sharon and I together wrote a book called *Family Illness: Chemical Dependency*. In the book we applied the model to chemical dependency. It was written from the outline of a course we were teaching at the University of Minnesota School of Public Health.

This book, *If Only My Family Understood Me . . .*, builds on *Family Illness: Chemical Dependency* and makes new contributions. It reinforces the fact that *any* stress becomes a family issue. Just as the family *as a system* pays the price in a stress situation, the moves toward solution and growth also are made within the family context.

The survival roles of the family members in a dysfunctional family, which are outlined in this book, occur in most stressful families, no matter what the stress factor is. The stress may be from alcoholism, from illness, from retardation of one member, from injury or accident, or from any other situation which can upset a family. When a family has low self–worth, the survival roles occur habitually and become rigid. These reactive personal behaviors involve the whole family system. The members are unaware that they take on roles. Most of all, they do not see the self–destructive nature of their role–taking because they are working so hard to maintain the balance of the family.

No matter how much we learn in theory, we learn most from watching our families. Through the study of family systems and family reconstruction through Virginia Satir, I have grown in appreciating my family heritage. Just as history contains wars as well as glories, a family's strength comes from the pains as well as the proud times. True appreciation comes from accepting family history as it is.

The family I grew up in would win no prizes for closeness. Through the years, each of us has grown apart. We live in our own circles of friends and relationships. We love each other. Our circles touch now and then. This is both happy and sad. I have felt total freedom in defining my lifestyle. I have shaped my own mode of living as an adult, as a parent, as a husband. Yet it is sad. I sometimes regret that I left home as young as I did, at thirteen. I sense a lack of family influence which could have guided me through uncertain times.

I left home to answer a vocation to Christ and His Church. There, I was intellectually and spiritually trained. Those stimulating years were so mixed with authority and a prepackaged program of study that I never felt much intimacy. Many saw me as friendly. Many others were unaware that they did not know much about me. The most explicit example of this was that I found it rather easy to maintain a strict secrecy about my plans to leave the active ministry of seven-and-one-half years. I lived with that secret for over a year.

I have been blessed with a colorful extended family. These are people I have met who have been influential giants in my life.

Virginia Satir is a person who speaks of the whole person. She taught me the meaning of "nurturing."

Wheelock Whitney is a renaissance man who has brought a health framework into the marketplace through his Minnesota Council on Health.

Irene Whitney is a woman who has a tender love for growing things. She is a catalyst. She is a change agent who sees existing needs and proceeds to make things happen.

Mary and Bob McAuliffe are persons of integrity. Study experiences with them about wholeness and chemical addiction led Sharon and me to develop the whole-person wheel.

My daily tutoring comes from my present family, from my wife Sharon, and from Pat, Sandy, and Debbie. I have learned from Pat's intensity and from his strong loyalty to family traditions. I have learned from the balance in Sandy between her independence and her wanting to be included in the family. I have learned from Debbie's courage and sense of humor. Spiritual development has always been a priority for me. It is a thrill to see each member of this family discover a deep faith dimension. They have all made steps toward a relationship with God through Christ in their own time. Their strength and trust have encouraged Sharon and me to be confident in our modeling.

Raising a family is hard work. Yet helping a family grow together is not just the product of work, blood and sweat. There are tears of vulnerability, too. While there is no magic, sure-fire formula for success, a family does not grow from blind luck. People are similar enough to prompt us to make predictions about family growth. By learning from each other, we can try to ease the difficulties a little by growing ourselves and by nurturing others.

Our hope is that the family members who read this book will become aware of their behavior and choose to change. A further hope is that the counselors who read this book will be able to guide families in a program of treatment which will rediscover the importance of each person, teach clear communication, nurture their self-worth and encourage them to the vulnerability needed for close relationships.

Part I
The Family System

The Family Mobile

The family is an organism. Its parts are interdependent. The members of a family operate in a system. A system is a body whose parts work together for a variety of goals: for peace and harmony, for efficiency, or for survival.

A family resembles a mobile. A mobile is a hanging art form made up of rods and string. Different shapes hang from each member. The beauty of the mobile is in its balance and movement. The mobile has a way of responding to changing circumstances, such as wind or the push of a hand; it changes position, but always maintains balance. The whole system moves interdependently to maintain equilibrium.

The beauty of the mobile in change is that even though the location of each member varies, each retains its place and importance in the balance of the whole system. Each member is important to the balance of the whole, no matter what the mobile's present situation looks like. A family has a similar tendency to shift toward balance. As families face the stressful circumstances of a new arrival, a tragic accident, an announcement of a life–threatening illness, or loss of a job, the family members shift to maintain equilibrium for peace, stability, and survival.

The efficient and effective workings of a family system depend upon three factors:

1) Each family member must have an awareness of his or her worth and importance to the family;
2) The rules of their living together must support each family member's self–worth respectfully in a humane manner;
3) Each family member must communicate congruently, that is, honestly with himself or herself and with others.

1

Within a family system there are smaller groupings according to age and interest. Each of these smaller groupings has its own dynamics and specialness. For example, the husband–wife grouping has its own intimacy and level of sharing. The specialness of this relationship is acknowledged but is not seen as rejecting any of the other members of the family. Members of the family system learn the many shadings of the words "I love you." The ways of loving are described with words like "I love you . . . as a father; as a mother; as a son; as a daughter; as a spouse." This becomes especially important as members of a system learn to choose people from outside of the family for acquaintances, friends and lovers.

In a system where differences are seen as opportunities rather than as threats, members do learn how to protect themselves from being hurt or misunderstood. A healthy system does not guarantee continual pleasantness and niceties. On the contrary, a healthy system guarantees that the members will be intensely aware of the complete spectrum of feelings. So a member of a healthy family will not enter the world as a naive Pollyanna, fragile and inexperienced with conflict. Instead, a healthy family member will have many tools available for coping with all sorts of feelings. A healthy family member will have learned how to deal with tenderness as well as anger, fear as well as vulnerability.

What Makes A Family Healthy?

There are more descriptions of dysfunctional family life and human relations than of healthy living. Disease is much more specific than health. In fact, health is rather elusive. People seem to identify more readily with dysfunctional relationships than with healthy ones.

Once people see their favorite defenses put into print, they feel a certain permission to continue their behavior. People say to themselves, "Look, if someone else did that, I cannot be too far from normal." The harder people laugh at the foibles of others, the more they are relieved within themselves.

Much talk about health is really talk about disease in disguise. Many speak of health as a means of preventing disease, a means of avoiding sickness. Inadvertently they become trapped into talking about disease in reverse. Health, like wholeness, is a very elusive reality.

Many speak of managing their stress and dealing with crises. Often the interpretation is to avoid stress and crises. However, stress is the norm. Since stress and crisis are just a part of reality, any denial of them is programmed for failure. So again, people are left with talking about disease.

Many speak of avoiding the dysfunctions in life which would contribute to illness. For example, people who hold in their anger and frustration may be leading up to stomach problems or arthritis. While the talk seems to be about prevention, in a subtle fashion the focus is still primarily on disease.

Power Struggle: A Fight or a Dance?

Power struggles can become destructive within families when they are perceived as disturbances. Often they are seen as something to be avoided at all costs because they are disruptions to normal, peaceful family living. If power struggles are perceived as fights, winning becomes very important.

In families of low self-worth, members' fear and secrecy become paralyzing ingredients in the family stress. Members react to external behaviors rather than respond to inner feelings. Their *reactive* behavior is prompted by one fearful member who tries to preserve the family balance at all costs. Such a dysfunctional family does *not* nurture its members' self-worth; rather the goal is to ensure the survival of the members' roles by rigidly maintaining the balance of the system.

System therapy is based on the idea that persons develop communication patterns that tend to protect their self-worth within a system. A person finds a communication pattern that best protects him or her in the system. The communication pattern is the personality that person begins to develop in order to survive. People learn their survival patterns in the families from which they come. They take this learning with them in choosing their mates and in raising their own children.

To speak of a family as a system is a way of describing the dynamics of people interacting with people. Often the word *system* is used to describe the many facets of a problem. Yet the same word can help in understanding the growth possibilities of a family.

People learn how to share and to be open from others whom they admire. If an atmosphere of open talk and of sharing things is modeled consistently, then a bias or preference for this behavior is reinforced. If someone who entered this kind of open and sharing system felt a need to have many secrets from some of the family members, or felt a need to hide his or her personal belongings, that person would feel uncomfortable. Not only that, the other members of the family would find it hard to make sense of this unusual behavior. This difference in style would have to be talked about in order to avoid messages of rejection.

If power struggles instead are seen as dances with different partners, they can be enriching.

Power struggles within families become ritualized very early in the family's existence. When conflict occurs, the reactions of the family members are easily predictable. Members say, for instance, "Don't bring that up, Doris will go crazy."

The ritual acting out of differences between members of a system establishes many things as matters of style. For example, strictness or laxity are matters of style. Loud arguments or cold anger are matters of style. Effusive, affectionate embraces in public or private are matters of style. As two persons dance together, first one taking the lead, then the other, each acknowledges the differences in the other. They compare differences and come to mutual acceptance without quality judgments. Power struggles seen as dances are enriching to life.

feelings
self-worth

Healthy person

Styles of Communication

Communication is the cement which holds a family together. The clearer and more direct the communication, the greater the possibility for intimacy. Communication between people who are learning to grow will not always be agreeable. There may be some yelling. There may even be some illogical notions expressed with passionate sincerity. To disagree does not always mean to be rigid; by the same token, to agree does not always mean to comply.

Communication within different families also leaves much to style. In some families, members never butt in on others. In other families, members finish each others' sentences, speak in fragments, leave much unsaid without fear of being misread or misjudged.

Family Members: Healthy, Dysfunctional, Chemically Dependent

Families are made up of individuals whose behavior may be described as healthy or dysfunctional. Dysfunctional behavior increases among all members of a family when, for example, one person becomes addicted to a mood–altering chemical.

The question arises: What are the differences between a healthy family member, a dysfunctional family member, and a family member with the specific dysfunction of chemical dependency?

The following three diagrams indicate the differences. The differences indicated also give some keys to treatment modes demanded by the respective situations.

At the center of a *healthy person* is the personhood where the self–worth resides. The most expressive aspect of the self–worth is the *feeling power* of the person.

Healthy people growing in wholeness can choose when to express and when to protect their feelings. This judgment is the basic part of prudence. People have the right to define the limits of intimacy for themselves.

As the diagram shows, defenses — shown by the small shields — are available for protection when needed. There is still ample room for expression of one's own feelings. Communication is twofold: expression of self and perception of others. This is illustrated by the dotted arrows, incoming and outgoing.

A healthy person can look at things outside of self and enjoy them. Outside things such as food, alcohol, work, leisure can enhance the healthy person. He or she is not ruled by them.

Dysfunctional person

A *dysfunctional person* is motivated basically by fear. This person fears being hurt by others. Most fears are based on the terror of being destroyed. This prompts a posture of protection. The large shields in the diagram show the large amount of time and energy needed for self–protection.

When one's whole being is concentrated on self–protection, there is little energy for personal expression. This is shown by the limited space available for the dotted feeling arrows. This condition limits one's expression of feelings, which forces others to guess those feelings and risk mistakes. The dysfunctional person loses practice in awareness of feelings, and thus often makes mistakes in perceiving the feelings of others. An example of this would be the person who periodically overuses or abuses alcohol, food, work, sex, money, or communication. That person's facility for maintaining perspective becomes dulled and inaccurate. Consequently, he or she makes mistakes and suffers excesses.

Addiction is a progressive focusing of all attention on a target, namely, a mood–altering chemical. This is an activity which preempts the expression of one's feelings. The freedom to express feelings is exchanged for the vigilant protection of the first love, the target of the addiction. The defensive shields become all–important. The small, very limited openings for feelings gradually become calcified with delusion. The dependent person becomes insulated from perceiving the feelings of others and becomes totally involved in listening to the echoes of her or his own defenses. This is shown in the following diagram.

feelings
self-worth

Chemically Dependent Person

9

Growing Together — in Health

What are the signs of health? People acknowledge their own ill health at different levels. Some feel they are sick with only a sniffle. Others need to be flat on their backs, half dead, and immobile before they will come to terms with their sickness. Soon the evidence shouts at them that they are definitely not healthy. Ill health, whatever the degree, is more easily defined than health.

Dysfunction, like disease, is specific. There are symptoms. There are diagnoses. There are treatments. There are prognoses.

However, for growing together in wholeness, there is a need for an *inventory of health.* A person, both for self and as a member of a system, needs to do more than *just avoid sickness.*

It is a commonly held fact that people are not perfect. There is no stigma about identifying with a dysfunction (especially in the privacy of reading a book). Some of our greatest humor is about personal and family dysfunctions. Drunken misadventures furnish the plots for situation comedies. The futile attempts of the less intelligent are grist for the mill of ethnic jokes. How many marriage jokes concern themselves with inept sexual performance? Writers, dramatists and artists have made careers out of describing the winners and the losers. The manipulators and the gullible are colorful characters for wrapping a plot into a story. Through humor, people give themselves permission to point at the inadequacies and shortcomings of others and, indirectly, of themselves.

Writing about a healthy situation sounds presumptuous. If health is seen as a static condition of being free of disease, then the description of a healthy "state" should come from someone who has "made it." An author should be someone who has found the secret. The underlying rule seems to be "Don't talk about it unless you are sure you have it."

There seems to be a yearning for modeling, for successful examples. A person looks for knowledge and insights. But the credibility comes from the example set by an author. For instance, a doctor had an extensive private practice in hypnotherapy. One of his specialties was helping people fight their addictions to food and cigarettes. His reputation was extensive. He treated many people successfully. And many people made effective changes in their lives. Yet there was always a tinge of doubt about him among his colleagues, chiefly because he was at least forty pounds overweight and smoked constantly. Looking at him and realizing that he had not yet made the same choices for health that his patients had, his colleagues found it hard to accept his whole message.

When we speak of the subject matter of this book, families growing together, one underlying theme is found in the process words *growing* and *together.* They are incomplete, middle–of–the–story words. They speak of an activity which is a commitment to struggle, a program of behavior following upon an idea, a fidelity to oneself and to choices made. Many issues are therefore incomplete, many concepts unfinished, for the reader must fill them in with his or her own experiences.

Myths and Models

No matter how many scientific books are marketed about parenting, they will never eradicate one of the major sources of learning about parenting. Parental attitudes are still formed by memories of how it was at home, old wives' tales, and hearsay. It is common for a father to shock himself by saying the very things *his* father said. They are the very things he vowed he would never repeat. What is lacking in scientific training for parenthood is supplemented by myths.

Two great myths about family attitudes are these: first, that parents are more important than kids; second, that kids are more important than parents. Each myth, once accepted, forms a set of guidelines for making value choices about parenting.

The first myth, that parents are more important than kids, is shown by some of the following rules of behavior:

- Children should be seen and not heard.

- Any conflict or disturbing information is shared only by parents.
- All important decisions are made by the parents.
- Adult activities take precedence over children's activities.
- During the summer parents free themselves from their children, perhaps by sending them to camp.

The second myth, that kids are more important than parents, is shown by these rules of behavior:

- Family money is spent for children's needs first. Leftovers are for the parents.
- Choices of vacation spots, of people to visit, of entertainment, of home furnishings, revolve around the children.
- If the children cannot be involved, then the parents will forego the pleasure.
- Children may have the privacy of their own rooms, but the parents must be always available.
- Home space, family finances, time, and even the music played on the radio become the domain of the children.
- Parents are not allowed to say no.
- Parents have to buy space in a restaurant or bar in order to have privacy.
- All of these things must be done with a smile so as not to traumatize the youngsters.

The behaviors following either myth are done out of love, out of wanting to be the best parent possible.

One Saturday morning the father of a busy household had just finished repairing a ten-year-old clothes dryer and was starting to paint an outside door. Beside him was a list of five other "Saturday chores" left for him to do. His young son came up to him, watching, seeing this familiar Saturday ritual.

He said, "I don't think I want to be a daddy. You never have any fun. You work all the time."

Parents provide models for living. Their lives are living exhibits of how to love, how to fight, how to decide, how to socialize. The greatest permission a teenage boy can have to cry is to have seen his father cry.

What parents do is live and let the kids watch and learn.

Parents are to live.... and let the kids watch and learn.

Signs of A Healthy Family

Each family member has:
- The ability to negotiate with other members of the family without put–downs.
- The ability to say yes or no without the price tag of rejection.
- The ability to ask without demanding.
- The confidence in the stability of the relationship.
- The ability to show feelings of all kinds without fear of losing the relationship.
- The ability to have specific relationships with individuals in the family.
- The confidence in the honesty of the family members, in feeling trusted by others.
- The ability to celebrate, have fun and play.

A family growing together is made up of whole people. Growth toward wholeness does not *just happen* to someone. Some try to keep a family together through outside incentives, like affluence, restrictive rules, and sometimes force. But a family grows together from within. Therefore, congruent communication and personal wholeness are the focal points of this book.

Congruence and Wholeness

The word "congruent" is a term borrowed from the science of geometry. When two geometric figures are identical, with the same measurements, they are called congruent. When the term is applied to communication, it means that the levels of meaning match the external expression of the message. Then the communication is called "congruent." When applied to behavior, congruent means that the actions follow consistently a person's view of reality.

Being congruent demands a basic feeling of self–worth. One has to believe in himself or herself enough to act according to his or her vision of things. The congruent person radiates a sense of relief and balance to others, with an attitude of straightforwardness that others may

occasionally find abrasive. For the congruent person is
not always pleasant, nor always regarded with warmth and
understanding. The value of congruence must be seen for
itself, and not as a means of gaining the approval
of others.

When someone speaks honestly and openly, it enables
a system to reach a certain balance. The congruent
person has a clarity which enables others to know where
they stand and then to choose whether or not to relate to
that person. Direct and honest communication is very
attractive to us, even though the congruent person may
stand for a totally different value system from our own.
The congruent person is true to himself/herself and,
therefore, open to relationships and further growth. The
congruent person has self-knowledge, understands his or
her own feelings.

Seeing and admitting reality as it is, even when it is
unpleasant, gives one a sense of worth. For example,
admitting inadequacy does not mean you have to hide it
from anyone. "I can feel good about being honest with
you. I can then feel good about me." A growing person
can allow open communication, can follow and give
flexible rules, can even tolerate mistakes and errors. When
a person feels self-worth, many outside things can
provide enjoyment. For example, a person with solid
self-worth uses alcohol, money, sex, and power to
enhance rather than to define who he or she is. Outside
enjoyments are a complement, not a compensation for
lack of good feelings.

The congruent person has the opportunity to take yet
another step — to *wholeness*. Wholeness is the
commitment to growth. This includes a spiritual search
for meaning. A whole person is not only in touch with self
but is yearning to find his or her place with others, with
God, and with creation. A whole person is not looking for
approval but is yearning to "fit" in the flow of things. In
this sense, all of the person's powers rotate around the
hub of his or her spiritual power.

Just as communicating congruently builds on
self-worth, wholeness builds on congruence. The chief
focus of the congruent person is that person's own

integrity, the system within himself or herself. A high priority for the congruent person is clear, specific communication. A congruent person values consistency between internal messages and external communicating behaviors. High-priority questions for a congruent person are these:

- What am I perceiving through my senses?
- What do I know about this?
- How do I feel about it?
- What do I want to do?
- What am I doing?

All people growing in wholeness are congruent. Not all congruent people are growing in wholeness.

A congruent person seeks integrity through honesty with self. Being honest with oneself, a creatively selfish activity, is the first step to growth. To know what one feels and to express it are important steps toward self-care. Some people remain at this first stage. But there is more — an even larger system for relationship, a system we call *wholeness,* for which congruence is a prerequisite. The invitation to greater intimacy and wider relationship is the invitation of wholeness.

Achieving congruence is the highest activity of the system within a person. Wholeness adds another dimension to the personal system, relating it to other things, people, and God.

I would picture it this way.

congruence:
honesty with self;
behavior and
ideals match

wholeness:
self in
harmony with
rest of
reality;
a growth
framework

The wholeness circle is included in the congruence circle. The overlap makes it hard to distinguish clearly.

Perhaps a couple of examples will help:

A man is very angry about something his boss said. He feels the anger through and through. In order for him to be congruent, he must give a priority to being aware of his feelings and sharing them. Wholeness allows him to decide how and where to express his feelings. In the bigger picture, keeping his job is also a priority. Stepping back, he may see an appropriate alternative within the larger context.

A man may be very sexually attracted to another person. Congruence would make awareness of feelings and their expression a priority. As a part of his wholeness, maintaining the relationship in which he is presently involved and respecting the relationships of others are also priorities. All things considered, he may choose not to make sexual advances at this point.

Obviously, the dynamic of decision-making always has an edge of uncertainty. Questions pull us both ways. "Am I choosing according to my priorities? Or am I just avoiding a risky choice? Am I seeing things within a larger perspective? Or am I selling myself out?"

To maintain wholeness, there is a need for an inventory tool. As such, the use of the whole-person wheel can be valuable. It will not answer all the questions, but it will help minimize the edge of uncertainty.

Introducing the Whole-person Wheel

Congruent communication — honest, open communication — is necessary for a healthy family system. It has an interesting by-product. The by-product of congruence with others is a step into the search for meaning within oneself.

A person is not only a member of a system which includes other people. A person also is a self-system — a system of energies or powers. Each power acts and interacts with all the others. Harmony within a person is one aspect of wholeness.

Each personal power has its own importance. Each exists along with the others and not at their expense. Each can give richness to the others. The powers within a person are these:

Mental Power: the ability to remember the past, to have ideas in the present, and to plan, imagine, and dream in the future.

Will Power: the ability to choose to do or not to do, to decide or not to decide, to follow through or change direction, to place values.

Emotional or Feeling Power: the ability to allow oneself to feel the highs and the lows, the joys and sorrows, the love and hate, the cautions and the vulnerabilities of life.

Physical Power: the ability to move, to be sexually active, to build surroundings, to feed oneself, to live in time and space.

Social Power: the ability to develop and maintain close relationships, to love and be loved.

Spiritual Power: the ability to search for the meaning of life, the meaning of the "I" that a higher power gives me. The spiritual power is the channel to a meaning greater than myself.

The following diagram is the whole person. Each section represents a particular power which all persons possess. It is a diagram made up of disconnected lines, because no matter how the diagram is drawn for the sake of clearer understanding, there is a need to note that everything affects everything else. The difficulty with a drawing is that it is static, unmoving. The system of powers within a person is very much in motion. It is a dynamic which is creative and capable of almost anything. The whole-person concept is explained more fully in Part II of this book.

What are the signs of health, harmony?

The life of those powers in the internal system of the person is a framework for growth. As with any system, wholeness is not a static condition which is achieved. Wholeness is not perfection which is attained, but is the balanced, healthy functioning of *all* the powers within a person. Healthy families are made up of whole persons.

20

What Makes a Family Dysfunctional?

A family fearfully facing stress and doubting its own worth is dysfunctional. The family members have feelings which they cannot afford to show. Yet they strive to act normally, while inside they fear that they won't appear healthy. Their communication becomes guarded because there are many feelings they cannot reveal. The resulting

feelings
self-worth

external
behaviors

External behavior with different protective messages.

double messages among the family members raise doubts in the individual members' minds about their own perceptions. Each insulates himself or herself, feeling that the others will not understand. The main resolution seems to be "hang tight." Literally, each member of the family finds a less painful way to survive this painful time.

The dynamic of double messages can best be represented by two concentric circles. The inner circle illustrates the reality of the person's self-worth. The outer circle illustrates the external behaviors used as protective devices. The congruent person has insides and outsides which match. To the extent that a person's external behavior differs from his real self, there is a double message. There is also anxiety, and a lot of energy is expended to communicate two different messages at the same time.

Defenses

When people are dysfunctional, their communication becomes defensive. Defenses have three functions:

1. To hide the pain;
2. To convince others that there is no pain;
3. To convince oneself that there is no pain.

Defenses are protective masks giving different messages to protect a person's self-worth. *The first function of defenses is to hide pain.* Fear of rejection and doubt of one's own perceptions are ingredients in a recipe for low self-worth. The pain that results is so great that it is tempting to hug the pain close inside as a secret. "If I keep it to myself, at least no one else will see. I won't have to admit it. Then maybe it won't hurt so much."

A person is often unaware of using defenses to insulate the pain. Earlier, there may have been an element of choice in the double-meaning message. With repeated use, the successful defense changes from a chosen response to a reaction as automatic as a reflex. At that point, there is no will power or choice left. The defense becomes second nature and has the irresistible force of a compulsion.

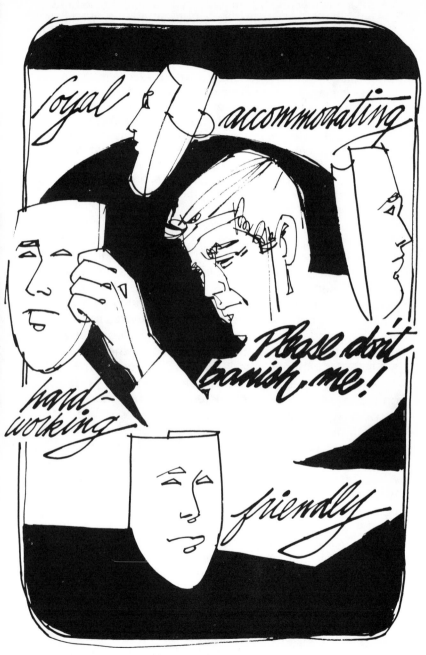

passive defenses to hide pain

Jeff is a young boy in junior high school. He admires his father, yet feels that he is just out of reach. While all indications point to the fact that his father loves him, Jeff has always felt a vague uncertainty, wondering, "Does he *really* love me?"

Jeff strives for good marks and for excellence in sports. He manages to earn acclaim in whatever his father admires. All his efforts are worthwhile only when his father notices him. Secretly, Jeff uses his father's approval as an indicator of whether he really loves him. Achievement becomes Jeff's defense. Jeff would rather expend effort of heroic proportions than mention his fear to his father. The pain which Jeff is hiding is the uncertainty of never knowing for sure whether he can count on his father's love.

The second function of defenses is to convince others that there is no pain. Defensive people, for whatever reason, engage in protective behavior. In effect, they build walls to protect their low self-worth. Defenses always presume an enemy. When the enemies are obvious, then the battle is simple. When I am not sure whether the other person is an enemy or not, I still need protective devices to avoid taking a stand, to buy time, to give myself room. The problem gets worse when I see suspicious, enemy-like behavior in someone who is intimate or close to me.

Defensive behavior, whether conscious or not, is based on fear at some level. Most defenses are not chosen consciously. They become a part of a person's style through repeated use. In fact, when low self-worth is being protected, the defense appears so speedily that it seems more like a compulsive act than a reasoned choice. A person with high self-worth, on the other hand, may deliberately choose a defense out of prudent caution before making a sizeable investment of self in another person.

A defensive person needs much more energy to communicate than a congruent person does. The defensive communicator must not only make messages seem clear, but must make them sound even better to cover personal pain. The defensive communicator must convince other people of the authenticity of the message. Essentially this person is perpetrating a fraud. The external message is not the real message. The external message is coming from the surface of a protective wall.

Aggressive defenses to
convince others there is no pain

Betty is a mother of three children. The older two children wish to stay out later than usual and to spend the night with a new friend. Right now Betty is unsure of how to answer her children. Usually she and her husband talk over most decisions. However, he is not presently available. Betty feels very alone making this decision.

She thinks to herself: "As a good mother I should know what to do, even without checking with my husband. Yet he is always saying that I am soft with the kids. He says that they can always outmaneuver me. But what they want this time does not seem so bad. If I say no; the kids will call me mean. I want the children to be happy. Maybe I will just let them stay out late but not let them stay overnight. Then my husband will know that I have not been too easy on the kids. And the kids won't have to receive a total 'no.' They won't like it, but I'm not going to get caught in the middle. By giving them each a half–yes and a half–no, I'll come out of this okay."

By giving all her attention to what the kids might think and to what her husband might think, she never allows time to ask herself what *she* thinks. Perhaps she has never thought to ask herself what her own opinion is. Her vague attempt at keeping everybody somewhat happy is the defense she uses to hide her fear and uncertainty. Her hope is to convince everyone that things are the way they should be.

The third function of defenses is to convince oneself that there is no pain. Defenses provide an echo effect; one shouts loudly in order to convince himself or herself. Each defense acts as an echo chamber. To get a reasonably loud echo, I must shout extra loud. It is tiresome to admit repeated failure. Almost anything looks like a welcome alternative to admitting inadequacy: avoidance, rationalization, changing the subject, and blaming others.

When fear prompts someone to cover inadequacy, that person mentally steps outside of self to check out the story. Looking critically at the story, the person feels good about it and concludes, "Why not believe it myself?" When the echoes of defenses drown out the ability to listen to reality, the person ends up not only being unclear to others because of double–meaning communication, but also confuses himself or herself.

Defenses to convince
oneself there is no pain

27

George is Betty's husband and the father of their three children. He works every day. He works hard. Yet he feels that he never quite measures up in providing for his family. Working harder helps sometimes . . . but never produces quite enough. The last thing he wants is to have his family find out that things are not as good as he thinks they should be. If only he could buy some time . . . He does this by convincing them of how hard he is working. He emphasizes his dedication by stressing the lack of support he gets from the family.

Over and over again, he comes on strong, loud and clear. His stories of working hard become his defense. His repetitions gradually become so convincing that he believes his own story. In fact, he believes his own story so much that he forgets all about his feelings of being inadequate. He never admits a mistake. He never says that he is sorry. By talking himself out of his fears, his exaggerated strength becomes that of a bulldozer on a rampage.

Understanding defenses becomes much more complicated when more than one person is involved. A person is not defensive in a vacuum but has an impact on everyone in his or her immediate system. Defenses within a family system take on the aspects of survival roles. They represent the ultimate in selling oneself out for the sake of balance in the family.

A counselor who recognizes defensive behavior in others needs some guidelines. One thumbnail rule is to interpret the client's inner feelings as *contrary* to the obvious external message. The counselor often finds hidden truth inside. The reason for this lies in the protective nature of defenses. To convince others of the truth of your defenses, so much energy must be put into the survival role that it approaches exaggeration. Over–compensation often points out that its opposite is actually true.

The chart below may be helpful in looking for the survival roles within a family.

WHEN YOU OBSERVE	LOOK FOR	YOU MAY FIND
illness alcoholism handicap accident	sadness pain being a burden being a drag shame	a Victim
powerlessness responsibility self-sacrifice	repressed anger	a Protector
success public approval rationality superiority ambition	inadequacy guilt	a Caretaker
defiance acting out strong peer relations	hurt misunderstanding	a Problem Child
quietness shyness out-of-the-way behavior creativity withdrawal	loneliness	a Forgotten Child

hyperactivity
attention-seeking
cuteness
humor
	fear of going
	   crazy
	fear of all
	   collapsing
		a Family Pet

friendly advice
"always available"
   stance
avoidance
prescriptions
	fear of client's
	   rejection
		a Professional
		   Enabler

To sum up, the best training ground for learning about defenses is inside yourself. If you know how you act defensively and what you are protecting; then you will know how to care for others more effectively. A counselor will avoid clients' attempts to trap him or her into becoming part of their dysfunctional system and will then be able to guide them to experiences of self-mastery through modeling.

Survival Roles in a Crisis

The Victim

Any crisis can produce a victim. Crisis, like any change, is a neutral reality. It is neither good nor bad. The root word for "crisis" means "crossroad." Crises lead people and families to crossroads, to choices for growth or for dysfunction. How a person negotiates through a crisis makes the difference between growth or dysfunction. Crisis comes in many shapes, sizes and circumstances. While each is unique to the moment, all crises have enough similarities to produce recognizable behavior patterns. Seeing these patterns of behavior enables us to make generalizations, learn from the past and predict the future.

The person suffering the crisis may be a young woman who dove into a lake, broke her neck on the hidden rocks below the surface, and now cannot move. Or he may be the successful father of two children who is told that he has terminal cancer. The person in crisis may be the man in a psychiatric ward who is told that he will need medication and psychotherapy regularly in order to cope with his anxiety. Or she may be the woman who lost both her job and her driver's license because of her drinking . . . and realizes that she is an alcoholic. He may be a prominent man in the community who, after a dizzy ride in an ambulance, finds out that he is truly addicted to his pills. Or she may be a teenager who overdosed on street drugs and learns in treatment that she is an addict. Each of these people is a family member with expectations, dreams and plans for the future. Each knows that at least a part of the life of the family system depends on him or her.

An added pain of the crisis is that the person who is directly involved is not the only one to pay the price. The lives of all members of the family will be affected by this tragedy. A crisis is usually not "deserved." It is often not deliberately brought on, even though there is always the haunting question "Did I do something to make this happen?"

Crisis becomes a stigma to the person to whom it occurs, a blot which singles him or her out. The burden is carried by the rest of the family, often in the form of a loss of freedom.

Elizabeth Kübler-Ross has done monumental work on death and the dying. She speaks of a cycle of grieving through which one passes at the death of a relative or friend. Kübler-Ross's cycle applies to the progression of feelings experienced by anyone going through any crisis. The healthy person — that is, one with high self-worth — is able to pass through the five stages of denial, anger, bargaining, depression, and acceptance. The stages are milestones measuring a walk through pain. In responding to the crisis, each family member goes through substantially the same stages as the person suffering the crisis does.

The first stage, that of denial, is the initial response to the news. "No, it cannot be." The mind races with lightning speed to look for some hint that the news is a mistake, a bad joke, a dream. But the truth of the news persists.

The second stage can be summarized in "It's not fair. Why me?" There is anger at receiving an undeserved penalty. There is anger at seeing the implications of the crisis on future plans and dreams. There is anger at the loss of movement and freedom.

The third stage — bargaining — involves grasping at any last hope, such as the possibility of medical discoveries or a miracle operation. The person fills in the blank of the following statement with a thousand alternatives. "If I do _____ right, then I will be okay." Everything from being kind to the nurses, to buying the very best care, to saying one's prayers correctly is the collateral the patient tries to use to buy a reprieve from this crisis.

31

The fourth stage is the depression which sets in when the bargains, all offered in good faith, fail. Nothing seems to be enough. The magic price is not found. "I'm stuck." It is hard to tell whether this is the lowest point or the beginning of a positive turn. One thing that is clear is that this is the time when the pain is felt at its fullest force. With the feeling of the unmanageability of the situation comes a deep sadness which prepares the patient or family member for the final stage, acceptance.

Acceptance, deep acceptance, is not the cheery "every cloud has a silver lining" kind of acceptance. Often this cliche-ridden reaction is just the opposite face of depression. Healthy acceptance is the attitude of recognizing what is changeable and what is not. This acceptance is a hopeful look at new alternatives. This acceptance carries a sense of hope and motivation.

For a person and the family to navigate through their pain takes a great deal of energy, congruence and high self-worth. A person who is protecting low self-worth is paralyzed by fearful defenses and will become stuck at one of the five stages. That person may spend a lifetime denying the accident, illness or alcoholism and may angrily and endlessly debate over who's to blame. Or that person may try to bargain away the crisis in a frenetic search for the normalcy of the past.

The rest of the family system tries to maintain balance within itself. If the family reacts to the dysfunctional person with loving protection, then they share the person's impasse. They join in the person's mode of operating, which is to shield himself or herself from the full awareness of the pain. To do this and maintain balance, they choose their own survival roles. Then the system's balance works not for growth, but for perpetuating the dysfunction. The suffering person takes on the dysfunctional role of Victim; the other members work to protect him or her and themselves.

The crisis could be illness, accident, injury, alcoholism, chemical dependency, emotional illness. The dysfunctional person is prevented from moving through the pain because the insulation of defenses protects his or her low self-worth. The outside behavior is a needed reflex action for survival. The Victim cannot afford to look at personal pain. The Victim believes that if his or her pain were allowed to emerge full force, the balance of the family system would be destroyed catastrophically. The Victim sees the crisis as a stigma. *The Victim's predominant feeling is shame,* as the following indicates.

As the rest of the family members assume their roles around the Victim, each looks for his or her own way of surviving in this pain–denying context. The roles are not static. They can be exchanged among the members. The roles are not defined by gender. Men as well as women assume the various roles of Victim, Protector, etc. An individual may shift from one role to another depending on circumstances. For the sake of balance in the family, the system needs to have someone fulfill each role. So in small families, one person may have to play several roles alternately.

Each family member sees the family crisis from his or her own vantage point. Each member's interpretation takes its toll on the person in crisis. For example, if a family member sees the crisis as a threat to family life, the patient feels anxiety. If a family member sees the crisis as bringing grave loss to the family, the patient suffers depression. If a family member sees the crisis as a challenge to be worked through, the patient may possibly respond with a sense of hope and positive motivation. However, if the patient plays the role of Victim in the face of these normal feelings, his or her denial system will operate and deny the pain. Underneath, the patient feels inadequate in light of the expectations presented by the other family members' feelings.

In a dysfunctional system the behaviors are reactive. Family members merely react to each other's roles. Much importance is put on one's own external behaviors, and the external behaviors of others assume exaggerated importance. Consequently, the Victim not only feels obligated to appear strong, but also trapped in a lonely corner with no way out.

In a dysfunctional family, members support each others' denial of pain and are locked into defensive reaction. Healthy families help each other out of denial.

The Protector

The Protector is the person closest to the Victim who begins to react dysfunctionally. This may be a spouse, parent, or sibling. As the Victim continues to deny the crisis and the feelings it causes and to use anger as a cover-up for shame at being "put into" this situation, the Protector also looks for a way to avoid the pain while responding to the double-level message of the Victim. Just as the Victim chooses to have outside behaviors give messages which are different from inner feelings, the Protector, for survival, builds an insulation of protective outside behaviors. The Protector sees the crisis as a threat to the balance of the family system. Intuitively, the Victim perceives the Protector's reaction and consequently experiences deepening anxiety.

The Protector sees the crisis and knows what needs to be done, but cannot afford to be open about it. The Protector feels obligated to act in the interest of the family, and so manipulates the Victim and others to keep peace. The Protector feels not only resentment, but also — when the manipulation proves successful — a sense of importance. The balance of the system is saved, but only the Protector knows the *real* story. Someday the Protector will use this to remind the Victim of the Victim's need for protection.

The Protector usually acts with the highest, noblest of motivations. The Protector receives the greatest amount of praise from others, even within the system. The Protector assumes the most important function within the system, that is, its preservation. If a Protector is gritting teeth and being a human sacrifice for the good of the system, then it would be patently disloyal for anyone else to do anything but comply with the Protector's aims. With all of these payoffs, the Protector finds it the hardest to see the Protector's role as dysfunctional or to make any changes.

While the Protector is motivated by love, his or her predominant feeling is anger, as shown in the following diagram. The Protector cannot afford to acknowledge the negative side of the crisis or his or her own feelings. The Protector sees the crisis as a threat to the system. As the

Victim becomes more anxious, the Protector's anger solidifies into resentment.

Helpfulness with an edge of anger demands relief. For the Protector, relief comes in the form of rewards. These rewards may be excessive eating, control of family finances, or control of family information. This growing control not only reinforces the Protector's feeling of being truly indispensable, but also prevents the Victim from learning how to cope with pain. The Protector needs a Victim. *The Protector has the contradictory job of keeping the Victim sick while doing healing things.*

The Caretaker

The Caretaker is the family member locked into feeling guilty out of fear of what the crisis will do to the family system. The Caretaker and the Protector often work in close alliance to maintain the family balance in spite of the crisis.

The Caretaker realizes, as the family responds to the crisis, that a Caretaker is much less important than the Victim, at least for the present. After all, much energy is spent taking care of the Victim, controlling family information and shielding the Victim from obvious pain. The Caretaker notices that many things are just not mentioned. One message is that the Caretaker is not important.

Another message is that this member, as a Caretaker, is very special. The family is proud of the Caretaker's achievements either in helpfulness at home or in success in school or work. The Caretaker realizes that such achievement gives some joy to the Victim and Protector. The Caretaker works harder than ever, hoping to achieve enough to alleviate all the pain of the current family crisis. The Caretaker, although unaware of it, is filling the self-worth needs of the Victim and Protector.

With the double message of feeling unimportant, yet being special, the Caretaker is left to make meaning out of a contradictory world. The Caretaker learns to interpret with top speed the wishes and needs of others. The Caretaker's perception is sharpened to a real art of anticipating the needs of others. The Caretaker's desire to be helpful is not only attractive to others, but earns many plaudits. The Caretaker becomes unaware that the guiding influence in most of his or her decisions is the external behavior of the Victim. Because the others in the system are locked behind their own masks of external behavior, the Caretaker never shares in the pleasure of direct communication. Because achievements never feel as though they are enough, the Caretaker is spurred on to more and more activity. The price is exhaustion.

Working for the service of others, putting the needs of others before all else, pursuing a whirl of activity, and keeping up the lonely search for some appreciation and approval are the price tags of this dysfunction. The Caretaker often enters one of the helping professions. Since the family members never took advantage of the Caretaker's superior insights in dealing with the crisis, perhaps other people will benefit from those "wasted" talents. The Caretaker who cares for others and sets aside personal needs often finds inside himself or herself many repressed worries — sometimes even a phobia — about illness.

The Caretaker tires of living with the double messages of the dysfunctional family system, yet cannot desert people who need a Caretaker. The Caretaker feels resentment that his or her special world full of promise did not turn out very well, but would never be selfish enough to go elsewhere for self-benefit. Most Caretakers usually do manage to leave the family system early. They go away to college; they enter the ministry; they join the armed forces. Their departures always have a respectable hero quality about them.

The Caretaker views the crisis as a loss of the family system. This makes the Victim feel ashamed and inadequate. One of the ironies of the Caretaker's development is that this kind of person often becomes transformed into a very good Protector in the family system he or she creates in the future. The Caretaker-Protector rarely finds personal satisfaction, is lonely with friends who are merely profitable contacts, is worried about all those for whom he or she is responsible, including his or her own children.

In the figure, notice how the Caretaker cannot afford to look at the pain of the crisis. The Caretaker sees the crisis as bringing a loss to the family system. The Caretaker feels cheated out of something due him or her. The Victim reacts with depression because of inadequacy. *The predominant feeling in the Caretaker is guilt for being "selfish" — for even thinking of wanting more.*

Triangling

The triangle in human relations is a picture of a system in stress. The triad or triangle contains the highest degree of energy for creativity and for conflict. The dynamic between two people can easily become ingrown, or a closed circuit. Add a third person and there are many more configurations for interchange. The third person has to be either ignored or creatively included.

The Victim of the crisis, the Protector and the Caretaker together form a triangle. They direct their collective energies toward maintaining the family balance. It is astonishing to note how this activity is shared in families. Most often, the Victim needs to do nothing except be the recipient of the crisis. The Protector and the Caretaker are thoroughly spent in activity which keeps the system working in spite of the Victim's plight. In effect, they take on the Victim's plight *plus* the reponsibility of responding to it. The Victim feels guilty for putting the family through this undeserved mess, but is unaware of being used by the Protector and the Caretaker to find their meaning in life. The Victim is usually unaware of the passive power he or she exerts. With the instability of the triad, a desperate rigidity is necessary to keep the family together. This becomes the major goal of the system. The goal of nurturing the self-worth of individual members is lost.

Family stress brings about other dysfunctional responses. They are the roles of the Problem Child, the Forgotten Child, the Family Pet and the Professional Enabler. The goal they all have in common is to find a place in relation to the main triangle of the family.

The Problem Child finds a way into the triangle by furnishing the family with a focus *other* than the major crisis. The Problem Child's "acting out" looks like an easier problem that must be solved quickly so that the family can get back to the "normal" job of coping with the stress of the family crisis.

The Forgotten Child becomes part of the family primary triangle by providing a relief. The Forgotten Child is the unnoticed one, the one the family does not have to worry about. The Forgotten Child takes good care of himself or herself and stays out of the way.

The Family Pet works into the triangle by giving the worried, serious family a pleasant diversion in humor and fun. The Family Pet's clowning does not add efficiency to family work, but is such an irresistible distraction!

The Professional Enabler is not a member of the household, but becomes involved in the family's primary triangle by giving the objective advice of an outsider. The Professional Enabler furnishes credibility to the work of the Protector and the Caretaker. The result is that the primary family triangle is reinforced in its dysfunctional response to the family crisis.

41

Some things to notice:

- How many triangles the Protector is in. The Protector feels much responsibility and indispensability.
- How many triangles the Professional Enabler is in. The central position of the Professional Enabler is important as a support to the Protector. Often Protectors become emotionally involved with Professional Enablers.
- The outlying positions of the Victim, Forgotten Child, Problem Child and the Family Pet. This indicates feelings of unimportance and loneliness.

The Problem Child

The Problem Child is the visible tip of the iceberg of family stress. The primary triangle of the family manages to maintain the balance of the family as it lives with the family crisis. The behavior of the Problem Child demands urgent, fast attention because this new stress takes too much effort to be added to the constant demands made by the family crisis. In fact, the stress from the family crisis has become such a part of the family's lifestyle that the energy loss it causes is not even noticed. The Problem Child's behavior is interpreted as a lack of caring about the rest of the family. The rejection of being thought disloyal is one of the main ingredients of the hurt in the Problem Child. *Hurt is the predominant feeling of the Problem Child.*

The hurt is compounded by jealousy of the family Caretaker. The Caretaker's role in the system is well-defined and well-performed. The Problem Child, who cannot get in, learns early that defiance is a good cover for hurt and inadequacy. The Problem Child feels, "If that is what it takes to be a member of this family, I don't want it. Everybody thinks the Caretaker is so great. They don't know what I know about him (her)." Any criticism made by the Problem Child is seen as sour grapes by the Protector and the Caretaker.

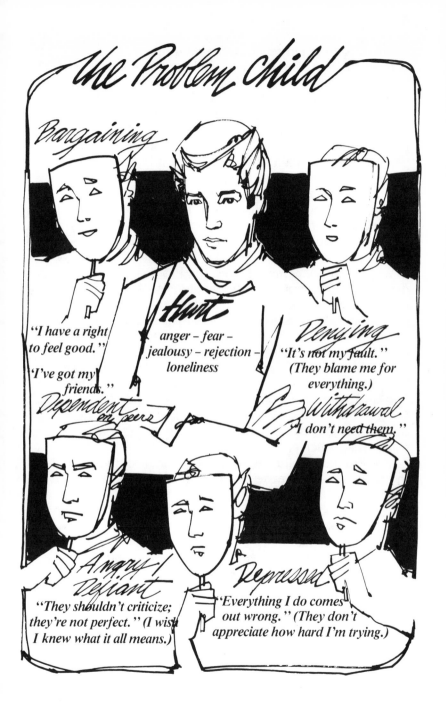

The Problem Child

Bargaining
"I have a right to feel good."
"I've got my friends."

Hurt
anger – fear – jealousy – rejection – loneliness

Denying
"It's not my fault."
(They blame me for everything.)

Dependent on peers

Withdrawal
"I don't need them."

Angry/Defiant
"They shouldn't criticize; they're not perfect." (I wish I knew what it all means.)

Depressed
"Everything I do comes out wrong." (They don't appreciate how hard I'm trying.)

There is a certain relief in receiving direct communication. The Problem Child receives a direct message upon beginning to act out the role. *The Problem Chid becomes important because of his or her destructive behavior.* The Problem Child may become pregnant before marriage, abuse mood–altering chemicals, or get in trouble with the law. Such behavior carries a double penalty: first, the pain of knowing that it is destructive behavior and the hurt of feeling inadequate; and second, having the behavior be interpreted as disloyalty to the family. What the family members do not realize is that their concentration on this new focus in the family brings a certain amount of relief from the stress of the family crisis.

What commonly results from the Problem Child's dysfunctional response to the family crisis is that his or her anger becomes frozen. This silent anger about the roles of the other family members is turned inward. Inward–directed anger produces hurt of such intensity that it demands some relief. The rest of the family interprets the Problem Child's behavior as disloyal. They, too, are hurt and angry. Little do they know that they have this hurt and anger in common with the Problem Child. Instead, the Problem Child feels rejected and withdraws. Sometimes there is the desire to make the ultimate withdrawal: suicide.

The Problem Child cannot afford to look at the pain of the family crisis because of a feeling of helplessness. The Problem Child cannot do anything about the crisis. Though expected to do his or her share for the family, the Problem Child cannot compete with the Caretaker. He or she feels inadequate.

The Problem Child, keenly aware of the manipulative communication of the Protector and the Caretaker with the Victim, considers them dishonest. When the Problem Child does criticize, he or she is accused of not caring about the balance of the family system and, again, is hurt and withdraws.

The Forgotten Child

The Forgotten Child has much in common with the Problem Child. Both feel unimportant in the family system. Both learn quickly that the prime energy and creativity of the family is spent in protecting the Victim of the crisis. Both know that they will have great difficulty in entering the primary triangle of the family. The Problem Child becomes the focus of attention through destructive behavior. The Forgotten Child finds it easier to become a loner. This is a relief to the family members because they never need worry about the Forgotten Child. The family inadvertently rewards the Forgotten Child's avoidance of stress by complimenting withdrawal as freeing the family from worry. The hurt which the Forgotten Child has in common with the Problem Child also prompts the search for short-term relief in solitary pleasures, such as watching TV, spending hours listening to music, using drugs, overeating, living in fantasy worlds.

As the Forgotten Child opts more and more often for building his or her own world instead of living in the family, this member goes through life on the fringes of the family's pain. Upon wandering periodically into the family system, the Forgotten Child feels that many things have happened since the last visit. Things seem to operate more efficiently without him or her and the feelings of unimportance hit hard. The pain of the family crisis seems so far away, compared to the double messages of the family members, that the Forgotten Child feels confused. This confusion develops into *contained rage against the crisis* which robbed this child of a place in the family. The Victim intuitively senses this and feels depressed about the lack of attention given to the Forgotten Child. But, as so often happens, once other things come to mind the Victim forgets this concern for the Forgotten Child. In fact, while everyone in the family likes the Forgotten Child, everyone also forgets to tell the Forgotten Child things, overlooks promises, fails to include him or her in the news.

The Forgotten Child learns early that the way to survive in this family is to become independent. The family communication may have double messages, but the

Forgotten Child fantasizes about personally being in charge of putting things in order. Such dreams sharpen the Forgotten Child's imagination to a point at which the definition between fantasy and reality becomes blurred. A Forgotten Child may relate more easily with imaginary friends than with real friends. In fact, every time the Forgotten Child tries to establish a relationship, he or she feels inadequate in communication. Confusion about friendship and sexual involvement, about disagreements and arguments, about possessions and materialism, trips the Forgotten Child into making many mistakes of judgment. The hurt of having to scramble back up again and again after such stumbles makes being alone look very welcome. In loneliness, the Forgotten Child learns how to reward himself or herself with secret pleasures, like food or fantasies.

The Forgotten Child cannot afford to look at the pain of the family crisis. Whenever he or she does venture a look, the Forgotten Child's lack of information and the chaotic nature of the family activity around the stress make even loneliness look attractive. The Forgotten Child's independence covers a rage toward the family crisis. While the crisis seems remote, it has entirely shaped the life of the whole family. The Forgotten Child has been rewarded for avoidance often enough to realize that rage is not allowed to be expressed. Quiet avoidance has become a lifestyle.

The Family Pet

Just as the Problem Child and the Forgotten Child try in vain to enter the primary triangle of the family, so the Family Pet never becomes truly included. The Pet has the added liability of confusion, because this person never knows exactly what is happening in the family or in himself/herself. This uncertainty from lack of communication or incomplete information is the Pet's share in the pain of the family crisis. With the large number of people already in the system, and with new information flying by, it often happens that the family members see the Pet as fragile, too young, too immature, and therefore not capable of receiving all the information about the family crisis. In this atmosphere the Pet becomes fearful that he or she is going crazy. Whenever the Pet mentions this anxiety, other members of the family seem to feel even more reinforced in their attitude, yet their words say that everything is all right.

Their double-level messages send the Pet into behavior geared for survival. The Pet's role in the family becomes that of distractor and tension reliever, through clowning, switching the subject, and nervous humor. As the Pet grabs the center of attention, he or she realizes that being in control of the action means that there seems to be more order in the world. When the Pet feels good inside, others reward his or her humor with their laughter. The Pet is on the way toward shaping a lifestyle of pain avoidance through humorous control.

Competition for attention in the family system is very high, so the Pet has to work hard and fast and will do almost anything to secure attention. The Pet learns that the best way to disguise the controlling, the interfering with communication, the taking over, is by laughing at himself or herself. Because others find it hard to be seriously critical when laughing, the Pet accepts the approval of that laughter and survives.

The Pet's outside behaviors are eminently successful at hiding the pain. But the price the Pet pays is the loneliness of knowing that no one really knows his or her true self. No one sees the tears behind the clown's mask. No one senses the panic the Pet feels when not the center of attention. No one perceives the Pet's sadness at the lack of intimacy. But the Pet survives.

The Family Pet cannot look at the pain of the family crisis without feeling confused. The instability of being out of touch is remedied by grabbing the center stage in order to be in control of the action. *The Pet's predominant feelings are fear and confusion.* The Pet sees the crisis as a threat to the system and feels that the only way to be included in the family system is by relieving the pain through a performance as a clown. This is shown in the figure below.

The Professional Enabler

When family members feel that they cannot carry on with only their own resources, they call upon helping professionals. As they are invited into the family system, they bring themselves — their talents, their training, their way of looking at things, their self-worth — with them. The helping professional serves as a guide as the family seeks wholeness.

The helping professional who comes from a position of high self-worth knows who he or she is, what he or she has, what he or she can give and cannot give. This person is willing to enter the system and become a temporary model of congruence so that the family members can learn new ways of coping with stress.

If the professional is coming from a position of low self-worth, there is a high risk that this person will assume his or her own dysfunctional role within the dysfunctional system. Then this professional's goal changes subtly from nurturing the members of the family system to getting approval from family members. If the professional comes to clients with a needy attitude, that person will become a Professional Enabler.

A professional may repress intuitions about the family system so as not to "lose the client." Meanwhile, things get worse. As things get worse the family members reinforce their defenses and the professional turns into a Professional Enabler who cannot afford to look at the pain of the family crisis for fear of creating more havoc. The Professional Enabler *loses faith in the self-worth power of the members* and mistakes the rigidity of the system's dysfunctions for strength.

The Professional Enabler wants to be a helper. The wish for competency is plagued by a fear of being criticized as incompetent. By wearing a "mantle of professionalism" to remind everyone (self included) that he or she is truly well-trained and effective, the Professional Enabler limits his or her perception of clients by constant self-inspection.

A Professional Enabler could be a physician, a psychiatrist, a counselor, a teacher, a supervisor, a clergyman, an attorney, a friend. Advice from the Professional Enabler is especially important to the primary triangle of the family – the Victim, the Protector, and the Caretaker. One member of this primary triangle usually invites the Professional Enabler to enter the family system because its members are looking for relief from the stress of the family crisis. The Professional Enabler's advice lends credibility to the work of the Protector and the Caretaker and reinforces their vision of the family. In fact, if the advice differs substantially from their view of the family balance, the Professional Enabler may be fired or discounted.

For example, a lawyer, counselor, or probation officer may be asked to leave if that person intimates that a member acting out the Problem Child's role is really trying to gain direct communication; that such acting out is not disloyalty to the family, but a way of entering it; that the predominant feeling behind it is not meanness but hurt.

The Professional Enabler joins in the family denial system by reacting to the external behaviors of the family members. He or she appears to be putting out brush fires while the forest is ablaze, scurrying around solving external problems but with the nagging feeling of being ineffective. Result? The Professional Enabler feels tired, used, drained, but most of all lonely because he or she has not touched anyone within the system personally.

An example might be the clergyman, who is always available to his congregation and finds himself called at all hours of the night. He is called upon to coach his parishioners' every decision. While they are asking advice, each seems to be seeking *prudent* advice. Later, with some disillusionment, he finds that his advice has been used as an authoritarian club to beat other family members into submission.

As the Professional Enabler becomes more dysfunctional, his or her own fear mounts. To be judged ineffective is bad. To be judged incompetent is horrible. In looking for a solution which will protect the "mantle of professionalism" and also have a possibility for helping the client, the Professional Enabler builds self-protection through reports, test results, elaborate use of jargon, or avoidance. The Professional Enabler needs the clients too much to terminate a relationship with them gracefully. Gradually the Professional Enabler's goal becomes finding the correct answer rather than leading the client through

51

the pain to new choices.

A helping professional may also become a Professional Enabler by working with an individual in isolation. Each person is a member of a system, and the energy and binding force of the family is so powerful that it cannot be discounted. Because working with one member of the family looks deceptively simple, one sometimes hesitates to open the Pandora's box of family stress. However, the Professional Enabler severely limits perspective by choosing to trust the vision of just one family member. There is the risk of looking for solutions to what actually may not be the underlying problem. Seeing a family member only as an individual, the Professional Enabler often finds that certain situations and behaviors just do not seem to make sense.

For example, a high school counselor may be working with a Problem Child who has discovered that one sure way of getting attention — negative though it is — is to cause trouble at home and at school. As a trust relationship grows, the student makes a few changes in conduct out of compliance. (However, it must be pointed out that the Problem Child will make changes only as long as they do not threaten his or her role at home.) Working only with the child, not within the family context, the counselor sees the child seem to improve, and thus withdraws, relieved and confident that all is well.

Soon the Problem Child is in trouble again, once more seeking the payoff of attention for negative behavior — both from the family's primary triangle and from the counselor. The counselor, who is a Professional Enabler, is left with the task of looking for a new game plan to offer the Problem Child, and the cycle begins again.

Regardless of the family's particular circumstances or the nature of the crisis, *the Professional Enabler's predominant feeling is fear of the client's rejection,* as the following shows.

Coping With Families In Stress

Many things, each in their own way, bring stress into a family system. Family members search for ways of coping with the pain. Any person who cannot afford to look at the pain of the family crisis will need defenses as self-protection. If these defenses are used repeatedly, the person becomes locked into a posture of dysfunctional reacting. These postures become survival roles.

Defenses often are below the level of awareness and leave the owner uninformed about his or her own defensive behavior. Incongruent communication among family members renders them incapable of maintaining relationships with others outside the family. Unfortunately, if a child does not learn to form genuine relationships within the family, that person may never develop that ability in later life. The progressive dysfunction destroys any future family systems, too.

To summarize, the family dysfunction is:
- *Personal* — it enables each family member to avoid looking at the family pain;
- *Environmental* — it insulates the relationships among all members;
- *Reactive* — members act and communicate defensively without thought or choice;
- *Uninformed* — members are unaware of dysfunctional behavior;
- *Self-destructive* — family dysfunction defeats the purpose of the system, namely to nurture relationships.

The survival roles and the family's dysfunction can teach much in the treatment of the family system. Treatment often brings about as big a change in the family system as the problem itself. Often the problem has had the luxury of long development, whereas the treatment is usually brief and concise. Consequently, time spent in treatment can be an intensive period of growth and learning for a family. And one of the instruments of greatest learning is the *awareness of pain* — the pain of secrets; the pain of guarded, cautious communicaton; the pain of loneliness. Because family treatment deals with a

family system, it will give more emphasis to the processes of relating and communicating than to solving the problems of each individual.

The general goals of family treatment are:

- To bring about acceptance of the reality of the family–wide dysfunction;
- To gain an awareness of each person's part in the dysfunction;
- To gain a commitment of each member to an ongoing program of change.

Group therapy and conjoint family counseling are the main tools used to move through the defensive behaviors to achieve these goals. Until defenses melt and a family member recognizes feelings, that person is unable to discover his or her own self–worth. Often a therapeutic system of people — a group — is needed to support as well as to confront. Then, like a mirror, the group will help the member look at himself or herself. At that point the family member will have the opportunity to learn and choose skills in clear, congruent communication. With congruence, he or she will not only assume a place in the family system, but also will see his or her powers as a whole person.

Working together in conjoint family counseling — that is, working with as many family members present as possible — encourages family members to share their feelings. As the members drop their defenses and allow their pain to emerge, they can accept their part in the dysfunction. They can proceed to rebuild a new system.

The family is a living organism. Through change and pain, it grows toward wholeness. There is never the possibility of going "back to normal." There are only experiencing, learning, changing, suffering, growing, building, and maintaining. Even though each person is unique, even though each family is unique, there is something about the cycle of birth to rebirth which gives people a commonality for finding a sense of meaning.

Diagrams of Family Survival Roles

When crisis strikes a family, its members assume survival roles in order to keep the family balance in spite of the stress. In the case of each role, the core emotion is different from the attitudes and behaviors the world sees. These survival roles are illustrated on the next two pages.

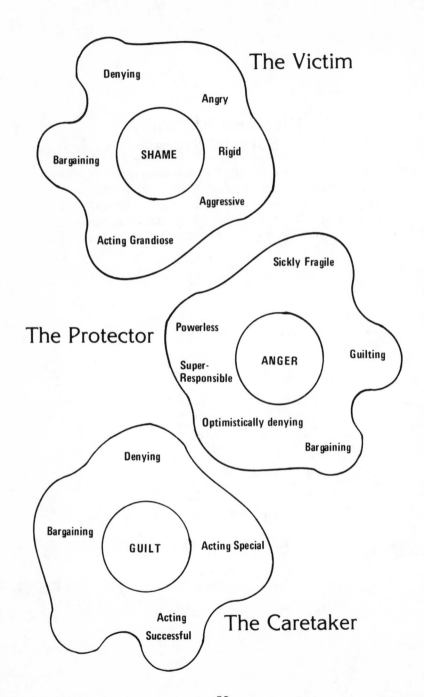

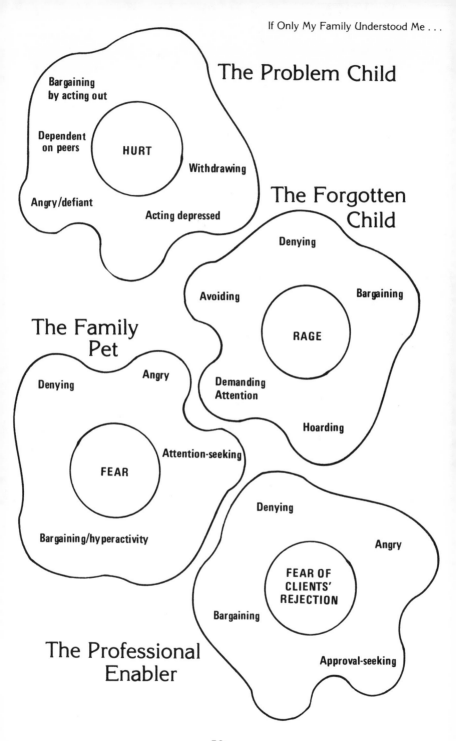

The Problem Child

Bargaining by acting out

Dependent on peers

HURT

Withdrawing

Angry/defiant

Acting depressed

The Forgotten Child

Denying

Avoiding

RAGE

Bargaining

Demanding Attention

Hoarding

The Family Pet

Denying

Angry

FEAR

Attention-seeking

Bargaining/hyperactivity

The Professional Enabler

Denying

FEAR OF CLIENTS' REJECTION

Angry

Bargaining

Approval-seeking

Part II
The Whole–person Concept

a family can find balance through stress

The Individual System:

The Powers Within

Just as a family is a system of individuals seeking a balance, so an individual is a system within himself or herself. A person is an ever–flowing system of energies or powers. Each power is an ability belonging to one facet of development within a person. No one facet gives a complete picture of a person. Each contributes integrally to a whole entity called a person. The Whole–person Wheel is a graphic and limited description of this concept. As a concept, it is a working manner of looking at what a person is. What follows is a description of a person's individual powers. Included are several exercises for stimulating the growth of respective powers.

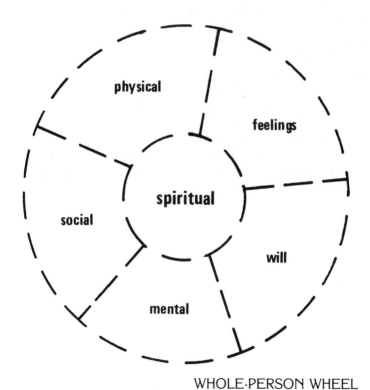

WHOLE-PERSON WHEEL

Physical Power

A person's physical power expresses itself with the body. The body can be seen as a prison for the soul and the mind. The body can be seen as a burden to be fed, maintained and cared for. The body can be seen as the avenue of all our perceptions, since we learn all things through the senses. The body can be seen as a spoiled child looking for pleasure and shunning work. Or, more positively, the body can be seen as the vehicle for learning, for expression of feelings, for giving and receiving pleasure.

Most of us would like to be either taller, shorter, fatter or thinner than we are presently. Since a person's performance standard seems to be closely related to body appearance, even grooming communicates what one feels about oneself. A person who, for other goals, pushes the body beyond its natural limits denies the importance of the body, for which rest is one of several essential activities.

How many books have been written about dieting lately? How many health clubs and spas exist for the trimming and tuning of the body? The current emphasis on fitness and nutrition heralds an era of giving the body its due, which can result in a remarkable growth in creative energy and mental sharpness.

Breathing, which brings life to the body, obviously is an extremely important activity of the physical power. It enables the body to center energies for concentration, for meditation, for exertion. For instance, a yoga enthusiast allows breathing to bring life and freshness, as the body seems to flow with the rhythm of life. Or, look at the breathing trances or movements of a karate student. The strength of the thrust comes with the exhalation of breath, often in the form of a shout. There is no need to know profound or exotic truths hidden in Eastern mysticism to recognize the effects of breathing: how about a simple belly laugh to release tension and relax muscles?

Muscle systems — all part of the physical power — are associated with strength, with self-protective actions. The muscles — which are similar to the non-physical defenses described earlier — may be kept in perpetual readiness against threatening acts, taut and waiting for some outside threat to trigger them into action. Of course, common muscular tensions — knots in the back, tightness in neck and shoulders, rock-hard calves of the legs — are closely related to conditions present in other aspects of the person's life.

Consuming food — not always purely for reasons of nourishment — is an important activity of our physical power. Food co-ops, nutrition and cooking classes, diets which look to goals beyond just thinness are all placing greater emphasis on this part of our physical power. Since gaining weight is regarded more and more as a matter of choice, a sudden upswing in weight often points to other personal dysfunctions.

A person's individual physical power may involve others, in sexual activity, dancing or massage, as examples — all pleasurable physical acts which carry meaning far beyond the acts themselves. The beauty of these movements is that they afford an opportunity for the person to appreciate the gift he or she has been given. When physical power is acknowledged in these areas, there is a chance for great pleasuring. When the physical power is linked with competition or performance, then the playfulness of it is lost, as well as the pleasure.

The physical power deals not only with a person's body or the bodies of others, but also acknowledges that the human being lives in space and time. Space refers to the surroundings one creates around oneself. Think of your grandmother's kitchen. What did that room say about her? In your imagination, you may smell cookies baking or soup simmering. You may see the coffee pot, always brewing. The surroundings we make for ourselves say things about us, messages which not only are conveyed to outsiders, but also — within ourselves — are communicated to our own feelings of self-worth.

Time sometimes is defined as something we do not have enough of. People remark at the discipline of the monk. Yet, when it comes to prioritizing how time is to be spent, his choices are similar to anyone else's. Time may refer to the pacing within a person, often called body time. In an effort to make more efficient use of people's time, and therefore to increase production, business management has been studying peaks and valleys in human productiveness at work. Individually, we pay attention to the same kinds of efficiencies in order to grow closer to our own potentials.

Exercises

Here are a couple of exercises relating to physical power. These, done in a darkened room to the accompaniment of rhythmic music, may involve family members or friends.

1. When all participants are gathered in a circle, eyes closed, direct them to move with the rhythm of the music. After each has settled on a certain rhythmic movement, ask them to open their eyes and dance their own rhythms until the whole group gradually becomes a unified movement. This should be carried out without talking.

2. A second exercise also involves rhythmic music, this time with people gathered in a circle and clapping. A person, designated as Number One, dances to the center with his or her own rhythm for a few moments, then approaches person Number Two, who joins in the dance, imitating Number One's movements until they are dancing the same dance. When that happens, Number One returns to the circle. Person Number Two continues dancing, now adding personal touches to the expression of the rhythm. Once Number Two has established a unique dance, he or she approaches Number Three in the same manner. This continues until all have danced and shared their dance with a partner.

After each of these exercises, the group may discuss what each person learned about the others by watching them dance. Participants may share feelings about dancing, about approaching others, about being approached.

Mental Power

Especially because our society offers many rewards for sharp mental power, this power brings us many good feelings. Scholarships and awards go to brilliant students. Only the top-ranking students in a class are accepted in schools for certain professions. The basic facts are these: All of us have mental power. Some have more, some less. But using what we have is a step toward wholeness.

The mental power has three aspects. *One aspect is in the past, in the memory.* A person's memory contains many hidden crannies, which may come to light as a new experience triggers a whole string of remembrances. A memory is useful not only for obvious reasons — like being at the right places at the right times and for remembering birthdays and anniversaries. Memories also are instruments for enriching relationships; reminiscing together can afford unique opportunities for self-disclosure. Memory also can be a valuable teacher since memory, coupled with feeling, is experience, and experience is the best teacher of all.

The mental power also focuses on the present through ideas. A person makes connections with past facts and makes new learnings. The idea functions of the brain are still the marvel of electrochemical engineering. A person is able to formulate ideas, lay out plans, investigate alternatives, and organize priorities. That is much more complex than simply maintaining a file of information.

The third aspect of the mental power is in the future, in fantasy and imagination.

The imagination, a world unto itself populated with all the creatures of one's dreams, enables a person to consider all alternatives, even the most bizarre. Fantasies enable a person to try on new behaviors. The imagination enables a person to try out new activities and explore possible consequences, to "rehearse" actions. The imagination lends color to logic, freedom to order.

Exercises

This aspect of wholeness, harmony within self, needs not only congruent communication with others, but also congruent communication within oneself. Self-knowledge — the sense of knowing one's true self — furnishes stability which gives the courage to approach another. In this exercise, best carried out with a caring guide, the memory is used to learn about oneself. These memories can be treasured for themselves or shared as gifts with another.

Early Memories
1. What were my parents like?
2. What was my home life like?
3. What kind of child was I?
4. What is my earliest painful memory?
5. What is my earliest happy memory?
6. What is the first conflict I felt?
7. What early spiritual life did I have?
8. What early sexual life did I have?

Grade School Years
1. How did I like school?
2. What were my friends like?
3. How were my relationships with teachers and authorities?
4. What was home life like then?
5. Did I have any specific problems during that time?
6. Do I have any sad memories?
7. Do I have any exciting memories?
8. Did I have any spiritual life?
9. Do I have any sexual memories?

High School Years
1. How was my home life?
2. What was high school like?
3. What kind of teenager was I?
4. What were my friends like?
5. What are my happy memories?
6. Do I have any hurt, resentful or fearful feelings?
7. Do I have any guilt feelings?
8. Did I have any sexual activities, pleasant or painful?
9. Did I have any spiritual life?
10. What were my values like?
11. Are there any successes or failures I can remember?

Adult Years
a. Work Pattern
1. How do I feel about my work?
2. How do I get along with my boss?
b. Dating and Marriage
1. What painful memories are there?
2. What pleasant memories are there?
3. What was the quality of my relationships?
4. What was my home life like?
5. Were my needs met?
6. Did I meet someone else's needs?
c. Children
1. Are there children in my life now?
2. What is each of them like?
3. What is the quality of my relationship with them?
4. Are there any painful memories about parenting?
5. Are there any pleasant memories about parenting?
d. Values
1. Do I know my values?
2. Am I compromising my values?
3. Do I live according to my own values . . . or someone else's?
e. Sexuality
1. How do I fill my needs?
2. Are there any painful memories?
3. Are there any pleasant memories?
4. Do I feel any experiences of guilt or resentment?
f. Death or Loss
1. Has anyone close to me died? Describe the experience.
2. Has there been any major loss? Describe also the feelings involved.
g. Drinking and Drug Behavior
1. Have I had any legal violations?
2. Have alcohol or other drugs caused any emotional pain in myself?
3. Because of alcohol or other drugs, have I caused any pain to another?
4. Has there ever been any physical violence to myself or others?
5. Has the use of alcohol or other drugs caused the loss of any relationships?

As I complete this honest look at myself, I may have become aware of certain high spots and low spots. Looking at myself realistically may give me the courage and energy to make choices and changes for myself.

From these insights, fill out the following list.

Assets	Liabilities
1.	1.
2.	2.
3.	3.
4.	4.
5.	5.
6.	6.
7.	7.
8.	8.
9.	9.
10.	10.

Every family has a history. Photograph albums, slides, home movies are virtual memory banks. Children love to hear parts of the family history again and again. They especially like to hear about the big events in the family's life, like the circumstances around the birth of each child; the time the family survived a terrible tornado; the time the dog jumped out of the car and almost was killed. Memories can weld a sense of belonging and closeness.

The imagination is the land of play. Much of the richness of living with children is in sharing their fantasy lives. Watching how children play house or, better still, joining in their play is to see them paint pictures in bold strokes of their views of the family. Children inadvertently give their views on parenting skills. Parents who are privy to these dramatizations have a chance to look at themselves in the reflection in a child's eye.

The imagination allows people to simplify or to complicate just for the enjoyment of it. What children do not know, they make up. In some games — like *Captain, May I?* — children delight in catching someone who does not follow the rules.

Family times, especially around campfires or bedded down in a tent or a camper, are the best time to play "What if . . ."

What if:

- You had the choice of any of the family's friends as your parents?
- You had a million dollars and didn't have to go to school?
- You could plan any vacation you wanted?
- Your house was burning? What would you save?
- You were on a deserted island? What would you want to have with you?

The "What if . . ." fantasies not only stretch the imagination's muscles, they also train the imagination to be a planning and dreaming tool. The imagination can be a faculty for visualizing alternatives.

Fantasies also help people learn about each other. If a youngster fantasizes about falling heir to a million dollars and imagines traveling, gambling, buying things, that child may be indicating an adventurous spirit. He or she might be a striking contrast to a sibling who dreams of investing the money and only using the interest for comforts and security. Even in fantasies, a person's values and ideas are evident.

Will Power

The will power is more than simply the power to decide to do — or not to do — something. It is the willingness to take the risk of going one way or the other. The key element in will power is not necessarily the actual decision, but the risk of becoming vulnerable by making a personal investment.

Setting goals and priorities, assessing performance, and overcoming obstacles are combined efforts of the mind and the will. Many people sell out their decision-making power in order to follow addictions. Addictions to mood-altering chemicals, to food, to work or to sex become appealing alternatives to making goal-reaching decisions, which often demands planning and discipline. Once a person becomes dependent, his or her allegiance becomes totally focused on the target of the addiction, which becomes the person's first love.

People avoid using their will power by cultivating compulsions, often irrational actions which gain acceptance by being present all the time. The compulsive cleaner, the compulsive worker and the compulsive eater never have to decide how to spend their time, money or energy. Since compulsions assume the rank of habit, they become second nature, a part of the person. Breaking a compulsion may require nearly superhuman effort and concentration. Think, for example, of the lurch of the right hand toward the left shirt pocket for the cigarette pack that used to be there!

"What do I want?" It seems like a very simple question. Yet it is one we hesitate to ask for fear of being selfish. Many people feel that they have too many responsibilites to others to ask that question at all. Or, in asking it, they look only for the "right" answer, for a polarity between good and bad, right and wrong. Of course, decisions can be made from this polarized framework. However, the more mature, the more self-actualized a person is, the more that person will be in the position of choosing between two or more good things. That is when we need more than moral guidance in making decisions; we need to rely on the more subtle part of the value system found in our intuition. Intuition is the sense of "rightness," the sense of "opportunity knocking," the sense of this being the "appointed time."

Many choose to let things happen to them rather than make decisions. If we empty ourselves of any decisiveness, dozens of requests and requirements will rush in to fill the vacuum. Appointment books and work schedules righteously dictate how we must spend our time. Circumstances and the loudest demands will gladly

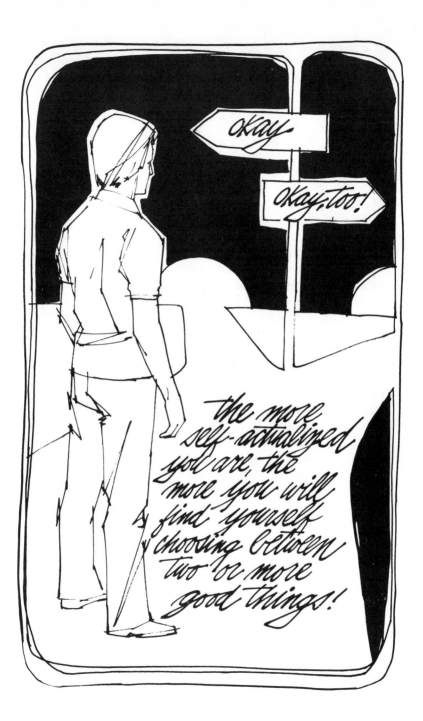

73

tell a person what to do. Some of us live by the myth that if we do not take an active role in making a decision, then we cannot be held responsible for the success or failure of it.

He says, "Want to go to a movie tonight?"

She says, "I don't care."

He says, "Want to go bowling tonight?"

She says, "I don't care."

He is certainly put in the position of power, namely to choose totally what will happen. He also is in the position of being totally responsible for the outcome of the evening. Consequently, he is left with a feeling of uncertainty and preoccupation. He may want to complain, but feels that there is nothing specific to complain about.

Some who play the waiting game suddenly find themselves in the middle of an unexpected consequence. The waiting–game people let life's occurrences just happen to them: jobs, marriages, children, crime, death. They create the mystique that since the world is too big to control, they might as well react in the most comfortable fashion possible with the least amount of stress. They feel that they really do not have much to say about how the outside world affects them. And at the same time, they lose touch with their inside world of feelings, ideas and dreams. Their passivity often looks agreeable, since they appear to be looking for approval. Actually they have forgotten their will power and avoid the risk of a decision at all costs. So they are the most surprised people in the world when those who love them become frustrated and angry at carrying more than their share of the work of the relationship. Lost in the fog of passivity, a waiting–game person looks puzzled and asks, "What do you want me to do?"

Exercises

Here is a graph showing the value areas of life. Values are internal standards set according to our ideals. This is our value system. Part of the tension of our personal development is in striving gradually to bring our values and behaviors to congruence.

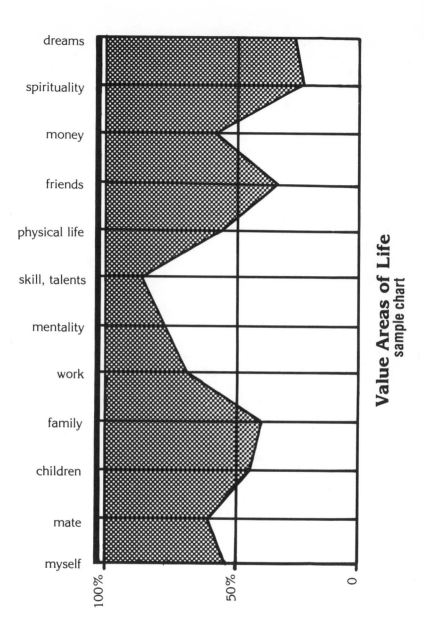

Value Areas of Life
sample chart

When we just cannot measure up to our own standards, we may have to look at our choices of behavior and find out what changes to make. On the other hand, we may have to look at the standards themselves. They may have been unrealistically high or inappropriate. When one's behavior and values are consistently different, there is high likelihood of anxiety, low self-satisfaction and low self-worth shielded by some defensive protection.

Consider that 100 percent on the chart represents the relative standard of excellence desired. Under each category, put a dot in the relative position indicating the degree of congruence between your behavior and ideal. Connect the dots and shade in the area between the 100 percent and the line. This represents the room for improvement. This is also the room for potential anxiety. That is the challenge.

- Where do you put your time, energy and money?
- What is the quality of your investment?
- Rate your performance.
- How much shaded area do you have?
- To make your behavior more congruent with your values, which will you adjust?

Emotional Power

The emotions are the soft underbelly of the person. They are the avenue of approachability, the barometer of credibility and authenticity.

There is no mistaking the softening of the eyes and the relaxing of the facial muscles when understanding displaces hostility. With the emotions, more than with any of the other personal powers, there is the possibility of double message. I may hear a person use the language of conviction and certainty. However, if the voice is wavering, if the timbre is flat, if breathing is shallow, if the eyes are shifty, if the complexion is flushed, then I become suspicious that there might be another unspoken level of communication present. Along with that suspicion comes a fear of being taken advantage of. Even when the data is not specific, my own emotions are antennae for judging credibility.

I might shake my head, almost scold myself saying, "I like the story I hear. The facts seem in order. Yet for some vague reason I cannot define, I don't trust that person." In our present world of facts and figures, the emotions are not regarded as definitive criteria. Yet, when honed to a fine edge, the emotions enable us to cut through layers of surface messages and touch the self of the other. Then we can decide whether or not to begin or to continue the relationship.

The emotions provide a sense of richness and color to life. Some people use lifeless, emotionless words to agree with others; phrases such as "I don't know" and "I don't care" are used to mean a half-hearted yes. We may get tired of trying to drag an answer from someone when our questions are met with these flat phrases, which seem to paint all circumstances the same neutral shade of grey. We yearn for that someone to show a preference with certainty and gusto — and, yes, emotion.

"Spontaneity" and "enthusiasm" are words which have much in common because both convey freedom, exuberance, feeling. Both are enriching words, yet there is an interesting difference. "Spontaneous" talks about someone acting from a power within, without constraint. The external behavior mirrors inner feelings. That person is congruent.

"Enthusiasm" goes into another dimension. It has a cousin in the word "inspired." "Enthusiastic" refers to a spontaneous person whose feelings are so intense that they seem bigger than he or she is. That person appears inspired, or literally, possessed by God. The word's Greek origin speaks of being "in God," making use of a divine power.

These two words indicate a large continuum of experience. A person can experience feelings from the depths of the soul. A person can also share the expansive feelings of a higher power. Feelings are considered to be optional equipment by many who tolerate them as "fine for those who like that sort of thing." To deaden our feelings through habit or addiction means that we exclude a vast part of the life experience.

The emotions have the functions of a hybrid power, joining forces both with mental and physical powers. The mental power is one factor, with its memories and thoughts. The physical power operates with its juices and muscles. *The independent way the body seems to cooperate with the emotions forms the basis for the lie-detector tests.* But as powerful as the emotions are, they are no substitute for the other powers. Although feelings may add richness and dimension to ideas, they do not do the thinking. Emotions, which call for physical response, for action, cannot be the sole ingredients in a prudent decision.

Looking at the wide array of emotions, we can know intellectually that they are all good, that they all deserve to exist. Yet it is unavoidable to see that some are more desirable, more pleasant than others. Emotionally, a person would like to simplify things into a good vs. bad polarity, which would cut down the amount of stress and the number of necessary decisions.

Some have locked whole sets of emotions into a closet, to be hidden from all, to be forgotten by themselves. Frequent occupants of these locked closets are anger, loneliness, inadequacy, hurt, guilt, fear, sadness — a mob of feelings demanding attention.

Feelings are facts. Feelings, like all of reality, have a right to exist, and reality is intolerant of denial. When feelings are repressed, they demand attention in devious ways. The emotional connection between stress and stomach problems is common knowledge. Research is showing more and more that the whole person becomes ill, not just one part. Emotions are similar to muscles — if you don't use them, you lose them.

People need to learn to reclaim their emotional power, to accept their feelings. Guilt, for instance, can be a healthy emotion for spearheading change. Shame is a condition in which one feels like an unworthy person. It is okay and sometimes desirable to be alone, but painful to be lonely. Anger is a healthy emotion and can clear the air in order to develop closer relationships. Hostility and sarcasm, which mask anger, can destroy relationships. Vulnerability can make intimacy possible. Self-pity can push people away.

Exercise

Divide a large sheet of paper into four areas. Write one of the following words as a title in each square: *happy, sad, angry, afraid.* Direct each person to draw, write, or scribble with colored pens his or her concept of each feeling. Each may draw pictures, make symbols, or just use the colors themselves to illustrate the feeling.

When the project is finished, have each member share his or her pictures with the family. The task of the discussion is to accept each feeling as part of the other person, to share ways of expressing those feelings appropriately, to explore the reactions of the family to their feelings.

Social Power

The social power of a person is the facility to make and maintain relationships. It does not refer to amassing lists of social contacts, nor does it mean possessing social grace in meeting people. The social power refers to the direction of a person's attention to others. A person uses the power while striving to look for, to choose and to enjoy other people in his or her world.

One basic fear in any human being is that of being wiped out of existence. So we look for safe places, for people we can trust. Mothers are very popular security-givers in our early days. Ways of getting wiped out vary from total destruction to minor embarrassments. In our search for safety and for a sense of belonging, we look for trust, predictability, care. Eventually, we people our worlds with associates, friends, perhaps partners. While our first goal was to survive against the "enemies," later in life we make an important discovery — namely, that the company of someone who freely chooses to be there is enjoyable.

A relationship is the gift of one person, inside and out, to another person, inside and out. The joy of a relationship reaches a new depth when one can say, "Even though I know I would survive and maybe even be happy without you, I want to be with you." A relationship

the meaning of a
relationship comes with the
choice to be together.

is an ever-renewable contract. Fidelity to one another is in being totally present each to the other.

To show the depth of our love, phrases like "I cannot live without you" or "I cannot be happy without you" come to mind. Spoken in love, the words carry the conviction of the lover. Such intensity demands expression bordering on the poetic; even then, words can only begin to contain the importance of the message.

In day-to-day living and growing in a relationship, there are many times that are not poetic. In such prosaic times, if the poetic words were taken literally, they would sound imprisoning. During times of dullness or of pain, the primary commitment is to struggle through the current stress. At times such as these, acknowledging one's individuality and power enables one to take responsibility for oneself and to allow a partner to do the same. People can withstand enormous amounts of pain when they can make some sense of it. The sense of a relationship comes with the choice to be together.

When the partners in a relationship are two whole people, something synergistic happens. The combination becomes somehow larger than the sum of the individual parts. A friendship develops, a couple-vision, a definition of the world with each having a definite place. Each knows that for the asking, there is another pair of eyes, another pair of ears available. Each helps the other to be more in touch with reality.

The life of an organism is a chronicle of movement. Movement from here to there, movement up, movement down. That movement can be geographical, emotional, intellectual, or spiritual. Each movement has the potential for being either growth-producing or dysfunctional. Movement is a part of reality. How a person focuses on the meaning of a movement depends upon the person's vision, self-worth, priorities.

People are born and they die. The coming of a new person into the world causes a change in perspective for many people. The newcomer makes a new system. What was once a couple is now a set of parents. What once were mother- and father-in-law are now grandparents. A budget which feeds two now needs to feed and clothe three. Time, space and energy need to be stretched to accommodate the newcomer. Who would have guessed that a being as small as a baby would take up so much time?

The person leaving this world also influences many people. One person's departure may bring relief to a family which has nursed that person during a long sickness. Yet death may be a sudden jolt to a young family when the mother is killed in a car accident. Another person facing death may smile, surveying a lifetime of accomplishments, and with a clear-eyed spirituality feel ready to go. There was a time when society admired the person who dealt with death through denial. Today admiration goes to the person willing to acknowledge death. It is even appropriate to express anger about the unfairness of it all and perhaps shed a tear or two.

Birth and death are the most obvious comings and goings in life. But there are many other arrivals and departures which have impact on forming who we are. A son comes of age and chooses to become a resident of another state. He is soon to leave the nest for a faraway school. A daughter leaves in marriage to make a new life, to find a new circle of people.

Today the divorce rate is climbing. Families blended through divorce introduce the step-parent to the system. A step-parent is faced with the questions "How much of me am I bringing to the family? How much will my coming change the family? Or am I just joining in and becoming a member of this preexisting family?"

The step-parent who wishes to be "invisible" and not "change" the family in any way has a lonely, impossible task. In effect, that step-parent does not wish to take responsibility for being present in this part of his or her world. Usually, this yearning for invisibility is really motivated by the guilt of choosing to fall in love with the adult member of the family. To minimize the effect of change may be an unconscious denial of it.

Part of a health framework is our acceptance of our history. There is a "before I was here," and there is an "after I came." The richness of the movement of family history can best be recorded through photograph albums, home movies and slides. Through such records, we

to minimize the effect of change may be an unconscious attempt to deny it!

Our Self is the tangible connection with the Life Force.

appreciate the transformation of a cuddly little girl, to the embarrassed teen with braces on her teeth; to the self-conscious young lady at the prom; to a proud woman standing tall, doing things, loving and being loved!

Spiritual Power

There is a motivating force which initiates, which ties all together, which directs all that exists. Some people call this force God. Some call it Cosmic Energy. Some call it Spirit. Others call it the force of reality. There may be many names, but all indicate a response to a power outside of oneself.

To the degree that one responds to the natural call of the life force, one experiences inner peace, inner joy, or, as some say, enlightenment. Life can be a struggle, full of conflict, meaninglessness and anxiety. Exploring the pain of life requires the investment of great effort. People exert themselves to figure out situations to cover all the bases, hoping to gain insurance for happiness and safety. The alternatives to exploring daily, visible realities is to explore the other part of life, the part that is connected to the meaning outside of oneself.

The spiritual power is the power of powers. It is the union of all that is in a person. The spiritual power is not found primarily through books, through courses, through academic knowledge. It is found within, through the exploration of the inner self. That self is the tangible connection with the motivating life force. Be aware of life. Listen to your breathing, knowing that as you inhale, life is brought into your body. As you exhale, life is given to other creatures. Or feel the heartbeat of another, wondering at the pulsating action which continues life within that person.

A woman who was dying of cancer in a hospital was visited each week by her parish priest. Each time pleasantries were exchanged, and serious talk and prayer were shared. An alliance grew between the young woman and the priest. On one visit, she skipped the ritual of the pleasantries and went directly to a serious request. Her voice was quiet, a whisper. "I know how busy you are. Please stay. I need to hold your hand a while." He stayed. During that fifteen or twenty minutes the shallow rhythm of her breathing was the only sound in the hospital room.

vulnerability provides the necessary openness for receiving the care

and concern of a loving God!

Then, no one could tell exactly when, the sound was no longer there. Her present life had slipped away. The priest had witnessed the tough yet fragile line between life and death.

After expending as much energy as we have, depleting all our strength, we notice that there is much more to do, much farther to go. The most real things to us are our limitations. At this point we become open to a discovery that is not the result of our own efforts. We find meaning through personal chaos. In accepting the inner life-force, we become receptive not only to the contributions of others, but to the acceptance of our places in the flow of things.

The discovery of growth through pain has two dimensions. One dimension is realizing that good things may happen even though our limitations are constricting and immediate. Another dimension is finding that our limitations force us to become vulnerable. This vulnerability is the basic openness needed to receive the care and concern of a loving God.

Happiness and wholeness and holiness, although not necessarily the same, are related. Human life is characterized by a search for happiness. But happiness is filled with paradoxes. To find happiness, we cannot grab for it, but must patiently wait for it as a by-product.

Happiness comes with being actively engaged with life despite pain and difficulties. Happiness is bound up with struggle. It flows from a life of purpose and service to others. That is why it can shine in the lives of parents facing mortgage payments, illness or job insecurity. Happiness is in the face of a young man in a wheelchair who is giving his energy to a worthwhile goal. Happiness is available to people of any race, color or age.

The spiritual power is the union of all that is within a person with something more, a Higher Power. Once the awareness of the life-force is internalized, all things are at one's disposal. Sunsets and churches with steeples, retreats in the woods and prayer beads, freedom in butterflies and a monk's disciplines, daydreaming and meditation, joyous singing and quiet prayer — all that rises comes together in a creative peace.

Whole-person Wheel:
A Communication Framework

There once was a very successful father who was worried about his nineteen-year-old son. His son wore jeans all the time, had dirty feet and long hair and wouldn't go to school or get a job. He seemed to enjoy being or doing anything to be different from his dad, which made his father hurt and angry. The father is a recovering alcoholic; the son smoked dope and drank on weekends.

During his first visit to the family counselor, the son, a hostile and rejecting young man, was very resistant. He did not want to be there.

The baffled father didn't know how the son had turned out that way, nothing like him. The boy, he said, was impossible to live with. When the counselor spoke with the boy alone, the boy said, "I'm a free person. I worked hard to get free. I don't follow or respect my dad's value system. I do things my own way."

The counselor said, "Free! You're as much like your father as I've ever seen a son like his father."

The boy responded, "How can you say that? I wouldn't work fifty hours a week like my dad, I wouldn't dress up in a monkey suit and tie every day. I make my own decisions."

The counselor said, "I know your father. I also know he is recovering. One of the areas he still has to work on is his rigidity. He is reacting rigidly to the pressures in the world he lives in. He wears the right clothes every day, has the right kind of haircut. He does everything he is supposed to do and he does it rigidly. So do you. If anything, you are a father-like-son team. *You are just as rigid as he is.* If you were free, you wouldn't react to him. You might have a short haircut, a medium haircut or a long haircut. Some days you might be clean, and some days you might be dirty. And some days you might wear jeans, and some days you might be free enough to wear a suit. You're a long way from being free. Your father used a mood-altering chemical to hide his pain, and you use dope and alcohol. When you can make decisions for yourself by listening to your own feelings, you might work toward freedom. Right now, you seem to be hooked on being the opposite of your father. You might start by being honest with yourself and then with him."

The boy said, "Help me. I'm so lonely." He began to talk of his fears, his hurt and his pain.

Two weeks later, he came again. His hair wasn't short, but it was shorter and neater. He was wearing a pair of brown cords. He had started in a part-time job. He said that he had sat down and talked to his father. They used the whole-person framework to identify their differences. They found that they could have the same framework, but that within that framework they could have many differences. He said it was the first time he ever really listened to what his dad said. He also felt his dad was listening to him. The differences didn't matter so much. What mattered more was that they could talk, listen, and learn from each other.

His father had said, "Physically, you are different from me, but if that's your choice, I can make room for that as long as I know you are doing what feels right for you."

The boy had told his father, "Socially, I don't really enjoy your friends or how you spend your time. I like having my friends over, and that's my social life and it's different from yours. I can understand that even though we have social differences, still I can learn to respect your choices."

During this time of hearing and identifying each others' differences, a bond of respect for self and each other was growing. *They felt closer than they had in years.*

The whole-person inventory can work with married couples, with parents and children, and also for one's personal inventory. It is also a way of evaluating the wholeness of counselors. Through this inventory, people can learn to identify and respect each others' differences. With this comes the realization that *they can have a common framework and yet be different.*

The whole-person concept is a growth process. It is a process of progressively owning oneself. It is a way of becoming aware of one's own energy and its many facets. As a person grows to wholeness, that person sees reality more clearly.

The behavior patterns developed by family members provide protection for each person's self-worth. The powers are the framework that we share, the tools each of us has to work with. People are more alike than they are different, and the powers are clear examples of people's basic similarity.

Practical Uses of the Whole-person Wheel

1. Personal Inventory of Resources
In the search for wholeness, there are innumerable paths to follow. The complexity of the search often causes us to overlook our inner resources. In order to arrive at a destination, we must know where we are starting from. The whole-person framework is a valuable map.

Look at each person power. Name three qualities which you possess within that power. State how these qualities are used.

2. Inventory of the Use of Resources
Begin with the whole-person framework. Look at each of the powers and answer these questions:
- How am I spending my time in each of these powers?
- How am I spending my energy in each of these powers?
- How am I spending my money in each of these powers?

Using percentages may help by giving a quantitative view of one's personal investment.

3. Inventory of Roles
Each of us has many roles: as a person, a mate, a parent, an employee, an employer, a friend. Questions:
- How much of my personal powers are spent in each role?
- Do I put maintenance and care of myself last after all other roles and cares?
- Am I gradually depleting and depreciating the very gift I wish to give to others, namely myself?

4. Clarification of Direction
When we feel directionless, confused, bored, or generally listless, we may use the whole-person framework as a

means of clarifying our ideals. Look at each power and ask the following questions:

- What do I want to do in this aspect of myself?
- What am I doing that does not fit into my ideals?
- What do I have to do to get what I want?
- What is holding me back?

This can be followed by a timetable for action.

5. Inventory of a Relationship

Whenever we look at ourselves through our own reflections, the picture we see is backward; we need someone else's eye to get a correct view of ourselves. We benefit greatly from seeing ourselves through others' eyes. The whole–person framework can be used as a tool for seeing ourselves clearly.

In a couple setting, each person fills out the wheel describing his or her partner. Each person answers the questions:

- What gifts does my partner have?
- How is my partner using them?
- What are the areas for new possibilities?

Accepting the whole–person concept as a growth framework means that any diagram of it on paper is really much like a snapshot of the person *as that person is right now.* It is capturing a moment in that person's development. We study it for growth and appreciation of this movement, of the *dynamic* it depicts.

Using the whole–person concept within families offers possibilities for self-discovery and the nurturing of self–worth. When someone shares a vision of self with another, both persons grow in trust. This trust can encourage us to risk being vulnerable, which makes a relationship possible. Such a self–questioning inventory requires clear thinking, honesty and specificity, all of which develop into a skill of communication. This kind of skill — straight, specific communication — is very much needed to nourish feelings of self–worth.

Epilogue

A family asking for professional help usually is in deep pain. There is often a feeling of failure attached with bringing anything so private as a family problem to the scrutiny of an outsider. The hair–trigger of defensiveness is an ever–present threat to openness and vulnerability.

Clinical experience would indicate that some hurting families are strict, loyal and traditional. Others are permissive, open and individual–oriented. One thing they *all* have in common is that they cannot effectively handle their stress. Each family knows that there must be a way of enjoying family life more. Each family is looking for a way of growth. Each family is not satisfied with mere survival.

Circumstances of stress are similar. Stress comes in many different colors, in various intensities, with no predictability. Life and death, comings and goings of family members, accidents and affairs, chemical dependency and addiction to work, illness and physical handicap — these form only a partial list.

Research is pointing out the interrelatedness of various kinds of disease. Not only the body gets sick; the *person* gets sick. Within the internal system of the person, all powers share the effects of disease, as all powers share in health. Likewise in a family system, the pain of a crisis is not restricted to one member. Each finds his or her own way of surviving. All share in the stress. All share in the healing and growing.

The particular style of family living becomes important only in order to discover how to best direct its richness. How a person or a system perceives reality depends on family history and a basic philosophy, and is really a matter of style. One family may set its priority on being close–knit and stable, with traditional loyalties. Another family may have a priority of individual growth and development, acceptance of differences as enriching, and a random communication pattern. The word "style" indicates a manner of living. There is no judgment intended.

People who are parents invest a large part of the busiest, most productive years of their lives in family living. With astonishingly little formal training, men and women generally put forth their best efforts. Their goal is elusive. But in spite of stress, in spite of differences in the way they live, they hope and strive to see their families growing together.

About the Author

Don Wegscheider, as Director of Faulkner Family Services in Austin, Texas, is responsible for implementing intervention and aftercare services. He is also Community Services Director for the Faulkner Foundation, hosts a weekly radio program on alcoholism and drug dependency, and teaches a course in family counseling at Austin Community College.

Formerly, he was Director of Human Services for the city of Coon Rapids, Minnesota, and headed North Suburban Family Service Center, a comprehensive counseling agency serving family members undergoing many kinds of stress.

He is a member of family counselor and author Virginia Satir's Avanta Network, an international group of health-oriented people invited to share in her work of nurturing individuals and families.

The author earned a B.A. in philosophy at St. Paul Seminary, St. Paul, where he also studied theology for four years in preparation for the ministry. Special education in his two main areas of interest — chemical dependency and family counseling — has included a summer course at Lea College, Albert Lea, Minnesota; two years in chemical dependency family counseling at the University of Minnesota; several workshops at Johnson Institute in Minneapolis; and yearly training sessions with Virginia Satir.

As a priest Don Wegscheider worked actively in the Twin Cities inner city areas for over seven years. He met many families for whom striving for family health was an uphill battle. His own empathy was not enough, and he felt a strong need for counseling skills bolstered by an understanding of a primary problem common to many families — chemical dependency. He found that a group of people supporting each other is one of the most powerful tools for executing change, for gaining strength, and for promoting health.

From 1972 — when he married — to 1981, Don learned first hand about "family systems" as a member of a family of five. During that time, Don and his wife, Sharon, co-authored the book, *Family Illness: Chemical Dependency,* a direct result of their experience as visiting instructors at the University of Minnesota School of Public Health. In a small booklet entitled *The Helping Professional,* Don shares their thoughts about counselors entering a family system.

Don and Sharon were divorced in 1981. Both are associated professionally with the Faulkner Programs.

Interesting Books

Bandler, Richard; Grinder, John; and Satir, Virginia. *Changing With Families.* Palo Alto, California: Science and Behavior Books, Inc., 1976.

Bernhard, Yetta. *How to Be Somebody.* Millbrae, California: Celestial Arts, 1975.

Self Care. Millbrae, California: Celestial Arts, 1975.

Gillies, Jerry. *My Needs, Your Needs, Our Needs.* Garden City, New Jersey: Doubleday, 1974.

Keen, Sam. *Telling Your Story.* Garden City, New Jersey: Doubleday, 1973.

Luce, Gay Gaer. *Body Time.* New York: Bantam, 1973.

Luthman, Shirley, and Kirschenbaum, Martin. *The Dynamic Family.* Palo Alto, California: Science and Behavior Books, Inc., 1974.

Miller, Sherod. *Alive and Aware.* Minneapolis, Minnesota: Interpersonal Communications, Inc., 1975.

Satir, Virginia. *Conjoint Family Therapy.* Palo Alto, California: Science and Behavior Books, Inc., 1976.

Making Contact. Millbrae, California: Celestial Arts, 1976.

Peoplemaking. Palo Alto, California: Science and Behavior Books, Inc., 1972.

Self Esteem. Millbrae, California: Celestial Arts, 1975.

Your Many Faces. Millbrae, California: Celestial Arts, 1978.

Wegscheider, Don. *The Helping Professional.* Minneapolis, Minnesota: Nurturing Networks, 1977.

Wegscheider, Don and Sharon. *Family Illness: Chemical Dependency.* Minneapolis, Minnesota: Nurturing Networks, 1975.